Contents

INTRODUCTION

My editorship of this collection of prose and verse snippets by and about my father, began as many good things do, round the family dinner table. We had been reminiscing about days gone by, and started to play: 'Who Said This?' which was one of the favourite games of our childhood.

"Who said: 'For living a Christian life, it is necessary to have a poetic view of the world'."

"Doctor Samuel Johnson."

"No. Nor James Boswell. Nor Queenie Thrale."

"Doctor Jonathan Sacks."

"Nice ecumenical thought, but no again."

"We give in ..."

"Cardinal John Henry Newman."

After some discussion of Newman's Idea of A University, the discussion became quite heated, until Pa got us back on track: "O.K. who said: 'The family dinner table should be a Table of Contents and not a Table of Malcontents'."

This produced general obloquy and groaning concensus: "You did!" "Quite right, but it is true nonetheless, so if you need to vent your spleen, or any other part of your inwards, then let's play One Line Obituaries'." Which was another childhood dinner-table game.

So we did. I forget the details, but it was things like: "She was born with a silver sock in her gob", or "the dawn of audibility in her stammering revealed a complete absence of coherent thought"; or "no one could have had a better opinion of her than I had ... and I thought she was a rotten, ugly, crooked little weasel."

Spleens having been thoroughly vented, we reached this suggested obituary for Pa, which he clearly liked: "He was always a bit of a fool. But he always knew Whose bit of a fool he was."

The evening ended with the customary suggestion that the random gossip of this table of malcontents should be the seed-bed for a book of family-auto-biography.

I had just had a couple of articles accepted for publication, so the medics and scientists all turned to/on me: "How's the editing going?"

That was how it all started.

This is how it has ended up. Or, if you don't approve of ending a sentence with a preposition, this is how it has up ended. Although, of course, not everyone would consider 'up' to be a proper preposition, and so it would be a good word to end a sentence with. Except that 'with' is definitely a preposition ...

That sort of fatuous word-play, I hasten to add, is not my customary literary style. But it is my father's style. His writings require palaeography rather than editing, since his texts are like palimpsests in which layers of messages are scribbled on top of each other and have to be peeled off to be deciphered. At one level of word-playing there is always, if not a message, at least a serious inference to be drawn. I once asked Pa what he thinks is the most important word in the English language, and his surprising answer was: "BELONGING: since it is at the heart of Christianity and has to be understood to be two words as well as one." The sanity breaking through, for me, adds to the fun. And fun has been my main criterion in selecting material for inclusion. I hope that my enjoyment prefigures yours.

'Sorto-biography' is my father's description of the book, and not mine, but I think it is apt because the editor of a traditional autobiography has to wade through thousands of pages of notes, diaries, letters, and writings to distil from them the essence of the personality behind them. But in my case I had only the person himself, and had to coax him to write down oft-told tales, occasional verses and some revealing anecdotes.

From the oft-told tales, I have culled a few to appear here; such as the story of Doddy's Charity Night or the Institute of Bankers Annual Dinner, or Pa's last game of rugby. Most of the poems are part of the family oral tradition of parodies, written to help us to enjoy our English studies. The John Betjeman piece is the verbatim text of a letter which was the reply to a query of mine for an article which I was writing on what is the best method to use in making the study of poetry 'real' rather than merely 'notional'. Some of the revealing anecdotes are versions, at my prodding, of stories or parables which I have heard my father tell in sermons, for which, as for all his speeches and presentations, infuriatingly for me, he has never used a written script. The pieces on 'Motherhood' and 'Hoarse Sense' and the poem on 'Looping the T-Loop' explain why.

Since I have started to write the occasional article myself, I have become increasingly aware of how few of my father's articles are available, other than in the archives of papers and journals, yet I know that for nearly forty years he has written at least one article every week. The pieces reproduced here on Smelly Feet and How Good a Catholic Are You just happen to be the two he was writing in the weeks when I began my task of editing this book.

The reason why I have not trawled through the archives is because my father specifically asked me to try to make this auto-anthology reflect the spirit of the people and things recorded rather than the letter: "For the letter killeth, but the Spirit quickeneth." There are, references to the main strands of the vocation which he has pursued, but there is no mention, or even hint, in these pages of most of the things which Pa 'did' in his working life as School and College Governor, Prison Visitor, External Examiner, co-opted educational representative on the City Council, Public Orator, National Officer of various professional bodies and associations, and latterly as Company Chairman of Moloney Search, but I hope that I have chosen a sufficient variety of texts to show something of what he 'is'.

If I have succeeded, then you will derive as much please from reading them as I have enjoyed whilst editing them.

If not, then I hope that you will forgive me, as readily as I am absolutely certain that he will.

Catherine Moloney. Brentwood. 2001.

PROLOGUE.

Thirty-five years ago, I wrote a 'slim volume' of prose satire and verse parodies, with a Liverpool flavour, under the title of 'A Plea For Mersey: the Gentle Art of Insinuendo' (Paperback. Gallery Press.)

In the intervening years, I have frequently been asked: "When is the promised sequel going to appear?" My answer has always been: "When I retire." I have now been very retiring for a decade and have accepted many bronze hand-shakes and assurances that the only offices I now hold are 'Emeritus': from the Latin 'E' = 'out of it' plus 'meritus' = 'deservedly'. The one exception being the Chairmanship of Moloney Search, my youngest daughter's head-hunting company.

Those who are sufficiently long in the tooth, gnashed and ground, will find included here, one or two poems and stories up-dated from the original Plea for Mersey to give this text what Merseysiders call: "A touch of neuralgia", without, however, turning it into a 'Son of Insinuendo'.

I hope that all who read it will find it a monument to the fact that seriousness of purpose with frivolity of approach is still the highest form of communication ... and the riskiest! If anyone is offended or slighted by my verbal risk-taking, please accept my apologies in advance, and credit it to ignorance rather than malice.

It is de rigeur mortis in a prologue, and that will give you some idea of what verbals await you, to thank 'All those without whom ...'. My special thanks for help, guidance and permission to 'rehash' previously published material, are due to Jim Parkinson of Gallery Press, John Emmerson of Countyvise and David Mahon of the Catholic Pictorial.

Especial thanks are due to Bernard Atherton for encouragement and advice backed up by his drawings. I think it is called "gilding the lily-livered".

There are many others to whom I owe thanks. Their identities and the degree of my indebtedness will be clear from the text.

I must, however, formally dedicate this parvum opus to my family.

THE UNFORGETTABLE WASSISNAME.

When Shakespeare wanted to express horror, he called it: "A deed without a name", so perhaps I should put names, or at least nick-names, to that dedication to my family.

The first thing which a religious leader, or guru, does when he recruits a new disciple is to give him a new name. This is usually initially a nick-name which gradually becomes a 'proper' name.

Which is why nick-names often give a better clue to someone's personality than their 'given' names, or even their titles. I once taught with a man whose first speech in the class-room started with the warning: " My name is Shufflebottom, and I wish to be known as such." Ever afterwards, by generations of pupils who had no idea why, he was known as 'Such'.

When I first started teaching, I was known as 'Kwaz' thanks to an early attempt to capture my students' attention with an energetic enactment of a scene from 'The Hunch-back of Notre Dame'. In the army I was known by the typically half-respectful semi-derisory title of 'Monk'.

As in most families, my wife and our four daughters have many pet and nick-names for each other, reflecting varying shades of affection and/or animosity. As a result, we only use full and proper Christian names on solemn occasions. For many years, Catherine, my editor, has called me: 'PODATUS SUBIPUNCTUS'. Why she should liken me to a small notational mark on a manuscript of Gregorian chant, I tremble to think, but I like the trivial gravitas which it betokens. And so, just this once, with formal gravitas, my loving thanks go to the five women in the family and to those who will carry on the family tradition; the next generation: Benjamin, Ruth, Katharine and Le Dauphin.

****

If you don't know the name, then initials will do.
Since all common people respond to 'A.U!'
And even the Queen, who is grander by far,
Has been known to re-act to a shouted 'E.R!'

****

DEGENERATION AFTER NEXT.

There is a temptation, in any attempt at sorto-biography, to produce an extended version of one of those school exercises entitled 'My Family' which teachers invariably inflict on their new charges at the start of each academic year.

I still recall, verbatim, one such effort by our youngest daughter, which was displayed on the class-room wall of her convent prep-school, for a parents' evening. There were several lines of glowing hagiography about 'Mummy', followed by a side-swipe at each of her sisters, and then this: "My Daddy is a sort of workman. People think he is strange because he wears a red woolly hat and does his gardening in the middle of the night. He knows lots of jokes and tells us stories about a giant called 'Goofy'. He cannot sing except for 'Little Mickey Miggs'."

Now, I hope that she, and all the other readers, will find these pages 'sort of workmanlike'. The giant called 'Goofy' had a large number of aliases, some of which appear in these pages. They included Saint Christopher, the Prophet Elijah, Socrates, Brother Juniper, Albert Einstein, Thomas Aquinas, W. S. Gilbert and G. K. Chesterton.

We still share the songs, monologues and music-hall jokes of my youth, though Mickey Miggs has had to be up-dated to satisfy animal rights' protesters. As have Tally-ho, Tally-ho, Tally-ho, and the anatomical version of L'Alouette which ends with the line: 'Je te plumerai l'intestin inferieur'.

They may no longer be politically correct, and they will never make the top million, but they are still good fun.

****

I refer to my spouse as 'My First Wife'.
It's a pet-name as everyone knows.
She's truly the first, last and only,
But it still keeps her up on her toes.

****

NUN THE WORSE.

I was expelled from my Convent Kindergarten round about my fourth birthday. My mother told me that it was for biting Sister Winifred on a Friday. Years later some friends who were Sisters of Notre Dame told me the truth. Which was that I had helped to celebrate mother Provincial's feast, in the presence of the assembled nuns, the young ladies from the Training college, the girls from the High School and the children from the Kindergarten, by singing a song, which was in fact an obscene Fenian ditty, which some mischievous distant Irish relatives had taught me when I had stayed with them the previous year in Silverbridge, on the border.

The sins of the father were subsequently visited on the daughters, during that stage of education known as: "Sister says ..." While they were still in the Prep. School, Catherine was accused of 'Vicarious insolence'. She had announced over dinner one evening that: "We did 'speaking in tongues at assembly today'," and I had advised her to ask Sister whether it was glossolalia or zeno-glossia. We're still not sure. Jacqueline was anathematised for spicing-up her Confessions with clearly fictitious episodes culled from the pages of classical popular romantic fiction. And Maresa-Clare brought home a message that: "As parents, you should be careful to scrutinise your children's reading material. "It transpired that during a search of the children's bags, Sister had found a copy of 'The Cosmic Christ' by the American Jesuit George Maloney. This was obviously my 'lectio divina' which Maresa-Clare had put in her bag by mistake.

Nonetheless, I took Sister's advice and checked the girls bedside reading. It was: Catherine: World Ballet and the Don Camillo Omnibus; Jacqueline: Untermeyer's Golden Treasury of Poetry and Little Women; Dominique: Wyndham Lewis's Six o'clock Saints and the Billy Bunter Omnibus; and Maresa-Clare: Willard Price's Volcano Adventure and Pride and Prejudice.

Dominique had to wait until after 'O' levels for her nunfrontation. "You did very well at your 'O' levels, "Sister said, "at 'A' level we think you should do Needlework, Biology and Scripture. With a sweet smile Dominique replied: "But, Sister, I don't wish to become a pregnant, vestment-making nun." And she didn't. She became a plastic surgeon. So perhaps Sister was right after all?

RELIEVE-O.

Children in the play-ground, fit to run and run.
Youngsters at the sports-ground, laurels to be won.
Off-spring on their home-ground, family and fun.
"Done Ya, one, two, three!"

Hard-headed business-men, in their pin-stripe suits.
Hard-hatted brickies' mates, with their muddy boots.
Hard-hearted check-out girls, couldn't give two hoots.
"Done Ya, one, two, three!"

Soliders in battle-dress, going off to fight.
Sailors from a battle-ship, passing in the night.
Airmen with battle-cry: "Conquering by flight."
"Done Ya, one, two, three!"

Children in a play ground, all too soon grow old.
Youngsters in a sports-ground, once so fit and bold,
Barely make their home-ground, when their story's told.
"Done Ya, one, two, three!"

Jack went off to Canada, Jill went off to Wales.
Bill went off with Tommy's Mum, Bert went off the rails.
Most went on to higher things, some went into jails.
"Done Them, one, two, three!"

Corner-stone of childhood: 'Get your GCE.'
Mile-stone in adulthood: 'Wed A.S.A.P.'
Head-stone in manhood, saying: 'R.I.P.'
"Done Me, one, two, three!"

REVELATION FROM MERE CHILDREN

"Daddy, daddy, daddy…who said God doesn't have flavourists?"

"Favourites, dear. Pets. Saint Peter said it. And Saint Paul."

"But they were pets. God always picked Peter first. I bet Jusdas always said: 'It's not fair'."

"Judas, dear. There was another disciple called 'Justus'."

"Well, if he was called Justice he'd know it's not fair. The disciples were not apostles who were the favourists. If he didn't have favourists, then why did he keep saying 'I have chosen you'? And anyway, if he hasn't got favourists, what about Heaven and Hell? Didn't he say: 'I will pick the pet sheep and not the pet ghosts'?"

"Goats, dear, goats. He said he would divide the sheep and the goats."

"…and the sheep will be my favourites…?"

"Well, not in the same way that Peter and Paul meant. They meant that he does not have special unfair favourites."

"Peter was an unfair pet. Sister said he paid thirty pounds to sneak into the priests fire-place and then said he was not one of his gang, even though he spoke with a scouse accent."

"I think Sister was making a joke."

"Oh, like Saint Peter telling Chairman Mao; 'You are the weakest Chink. Go to Murgatroyd'?"

"Purgatory, dear. Yes something like that."

"If God didn't have favourites, He wouldn't have to send people to purgatory. Sister has pets and they get off having to practice abstention."

"Detention, dear. 'Abstention' means to stop doing things…"

"That's right, they have to stop…"

"No, dear, 'detention' is being kept in from play."

"Like murgatory?"

"Well, sort of like purgatory. But purgatory is more like going to the hairdressers to get ready before you go to a big party. When God chooses people like Peter and Paul, or you and me, for special jobs he gives them hard things to do but promises lovely prizes at the end. If I give your big strong brother a hard gardening job, and your little sister an easy kitchen job…"

"And make me wash the car…"

"And allow you to help me wash the car…and then I give you all the same treat at the end, am I being fair or unfair?"

"I bet I have to 'Help God' to wash cars in purgatroyd for ever and ever amen. And wash the goats as well. Anyway, who is Chris Ogonous?"

"I have a very important newspaper to read, now you run along and ask your Mummy…"

"Mummy, mummy, mummy…"

A DIP IN THE GENE POOL.

My Father was a G.P. in the days when all General Medical Practitioners were divided into 'pooh-poohs' and 'wind-uppers'.

He was a pooh-pooh-with-style, being widely read in poetry and literature, as well as theology. He was also Apostolic Syndic to the Franciscan Friars Minor in Liverpool. His conversation was a glorious mixture of literature, religion, medicine and mischief. When I first read the Bible, Shakespeare, the Romantic poets, and the classical novels of English fiction, I was amazed to find that they were full of quotations from my Father. Or rather, to be exact, of mis-quotations from my Father, who was wont to adapt his quotes to the appropriate times and moments. I was frequently chastised in later years by English teachers who took the naivety of my literary inheritance to be insolence. I really believed, for instance, that Macauley had written: "How can man die better than facing fearful sods."

Like many G.Ps he claimed that he never treated individuals, only families. At his city-centre surgery there was constant family chat, redolent of the linguistic idiosyncratic felicity of scouse patients. He was fluent in the vernacular. He would never call: "Stress evacuation" what a patient had referred to as: "A touch ev the trots." A lady who told him that she was recovering from: "A operation for a hysterical rectum," found herself consoled with a suitable text from: "The epistle to the fallopians."

Many of his patients actually believed that the father of the N.H.S. was called Urinary Bevan. He would have enjoyed the consternation caused to surgical patients, on their way to theatre in a local hospital recently, by a large poster on the wall which cautioned:

WARNING: SECURITY GUARDS OPERATE IN THIS HOSPITAL.

He often gave voice to medical ditties, in what he called an 'organ recital'. He also, occasionally performed his own version of classics like 'Gunga Din' or 'Lepanto' or 'Horatius at the Bridge' from the Lays of Ancient Rome. His versions were a mixture of music-hall ballad and drawing-room political satire. I've tried to catch the spirit in the next couple of pages, written during an NHS crisis, at the time of the 1999 Kensington and Chelsea bye-election:-

CURARE. OH.OH.OH.OH.

An anaesthetist Tutor and Prof.
Was renowned for the way he would scoff.
At his Houseman he'd leer,
With a cynical sneer,
And say: "Pierce with a pin and push off!"

PARTY POOPER.

She complained of a pain in her belly.
Her Mum said: "She's spewin the welly."
Her stool soon revealed
Party remnants congealed:
Salmonella, E-Coli, and Jelly.

PUNCTUATED SPLEEN.

"You've got a disease of the colon.
We're going to do a big op.
If we don't you'll lapse into a comma,
And grind to a total full-stop."

MISTAKE AND KIDNEY.

A nephritic consultant, when spiteful,
Claimed: "My laperoscope's not insightful."
But a miss is as good as a mylogram, folks.
So, it's blood from a stone."
Oh, how frightful!

CHANGEABLE WHETHER.

All hail to Organ Donors.
Who give up their kidneys or hearts.
And blessings to the weather girl.
Who says: "Rain is spreading tall parts".

ON AN ELECTORAL ROLL.

Mike Portillo of Kensingston, to the nine hacks he swore,
That the great House of Commons should suffer loss no more.
To the Chief Whip he swore it, and named a polling day,
And bade his canvassers ride forth,
East and West and South and North, to summon straight and gay.

Election leaflets filled the streets, competing with the litter.
And cabbies plugged the candidate that they considered fitter.
Reluctant hands were shaken. Bald infant heads were pat.
While to each blue-rinsed matron, Portillo doffed his hat.

The Vestal Virgins, Chelsea Branch, forth sallied to Whitehall,
Lest the safest seat in Torydom should be about to fall.
With the Lares and Penates of the Lower House in tow,
They lectured all the waverers, and told the belles of Bow.

From on the Coliseum steps, where all the plebs could see,
Portillo shouted: "Who will stand on either hand with me?"
Then up spake Archie Norman, an Asda man was he.
"Yea I will pledge my supermarket forces all for thee."
And who came stoutly to his left? Anne Widdicombe no less.
To all the gels of Kensington a modern Good Queen Bess.

"Hague bless him," quoth spin-doctors," "and win him back his seat.
Through sleaze and slur and sound-bites, a quite prodigious feat."
"Blair curse him," railed the focus-group, "and cart him to the tower.
With Ashcroft and with Robinson and all that motley shower.
And while they're busy at it, and all marching off to Hell,
They could do us all a favour, and take Livingstone as well."

And the story is still told, in M. Fayed's Knightsbridge store,
Of how Portcullis took this seat in the brave days of yore.
Alas for Portillistas, his victory was brief.
Within a year he'd got the heave, and I.D.S. was chief.

X-RAYSED EXPECTATIONS.

Whilst at University, I had tried a variety of part-time vacation jobs: postman, librarian, life-guard, docker, pea-viner, and so on, but the one that changed my life was the one I did between demob from the army, in the Spring of 1958, after a national service extended to nearly three years, and starting to teach in the Autumn.

One Sunday morning, I was in Blessed Sacrament church in Aintree with my brothers, when I noticed a trio of very attractive young ladies who were new to the parish. Indiscreet inquiries revealed that they were Irish student radiographers 'come across' to train at Fazakerly and Aintree hospital.

So, early the next morning, I presented myself at Matron's office, to offer my services as a gardener. Instead, I was offered a temporary job as an Orderly on East Upper which was part of the TB isolation unit in the Aintree Hospital. "East Upper is a TB ward, so I'll need a precautionary chest X-Ray, won't I?" I suggested. Shortly afterwards, I was standing, stripped to the waist, in front of the X-Ray machine, when a gentle lilting voice said: "Breathe in, hold it, thank you."

I had, and still have, an enormous respect for those who follow the vocation of nursing. I remember my Mother's tales of her days in Walton Hospital when it was one of the biggest in Europe, and the nurses worked as many hours as it took, and were paid nearly enough to cover their laundry bills. But, though I didn't mind traipsing after Matron, Sister, Nurse and Matron's Dog, on ward rounds, and though I was awarded the 'Sputum Cup of the Year Award' before I left, I clearly lacked the requisite bed-pan manner for the profession.

Noelene continued as a part-time radiographer, with intervals for having four girls, at the Oxford Road Maternity Hospital and the Royal Liverpool Women's Hospital until last year, when she finally hung up her lead apron, and allowed me to breathe out.

She still maintains that I looked alright from the back.

THE ROAD TO THE AISLES.

Noelene's gentle Irish lilt remains. She says that my attempts at an Irish accent always turn into stage Scottish. It could be. Och Aye. Begorrah. The Noo.

I was shopping with her one day in a supermarket. She had wandered off with her trolley and I was strolling about aimlessly. A fussy young lady in a uniform-dress accosted me: "Can I help you, Sir?" Looking up-and-down the nearest aisle for my missing spouse, I exclaimed, with a sigh: "The Thane of Fife had a wife. Where is she now?" Then the curse of the Scottish Play struck. The Assistant scuttled off. Minutes later, there was an announcement over the tannoy system: "Would Mrs. Thane please come to the Personnel Office?" As I fled, the words of the famous kosher Scottish poet, Rabbi Burns, were running through my head.

TAM O'TESCS

Whan her's stood droolin ower fruit,
Aboot which ye don't give a hoot.
An rooten right across the aisle,
An, nagnagnagen all the while.

"Try if they breeks wal fit yer hurdien.
Stap leering at the stacking burdies.
Help me to change yon mini-sark.
It maks ma tatoos look too dark.
Some cheese should no be hard to find.
Mak sure ye get a well-kent kind.
Last week, I mind, ya towzie man,
Ya bought a stodge of parmesan.
Way past its sell-by date an aw.
Lak you yersel. But 'Best Before'.
Put back them bottles, and those fags.
Grab me a trolley, hold these bags.
Give me your cash, I need much more.
That's all I ever want you for ..."

She wanders off, still prating on,
Now you relax, at last she's gone.

If then tae roam, ye are inclined,
An checkoot girls run in yer mind.
Tak my advice an run lak Hell.
An leave yer spouse tae Personnel.

FERTILITY RIGHTS.

Way back in the 1950's I was a Probationer Teacher in an all-age school in Toxteth. It was the Headmaster's practice, on Friday afternoons, to take over my class and send me off to the Staff-room with a copy of the latest educational research to study and assess.

One Friday, he handed me the doctoral dissertation of a local student, John Baron Mays, who subsequently became a Professor of Sociology at Liverpool University. In this thesis, which was later published under the title of 'Growing Up in the City', he described the boys I was teaching as: "The unwanted by-product of an overindulged sexual appetite." I was naïve enough to be shocked, and realist enough to be depressed.

Later, I was making my way home, or, as they used to say in Toxteth: 'Declaring U.D.I.' which stands for 'up de 'ill', when I passed a tenement block. Inside the railings on the ground floor, sat an elderly woman in an old rocking chair. She had a child in her arms; another on her lap; two more at her feet: and a veritable posse of lads standing around.

As I drew alongside her, she gave me a huge smile, pointed expansively to her vast brood, held up the infant to be admired, and said, proudly: "Ah, God, if you 'ad ten and then a wooden one, you'd still love it wouldn't you?" I was naïve enough to be elated and idealist enough to be exhilarated.

Even the 'latch-key kids' in those days had three supportive relatives' "Me Mam, me Nin, an me Auntie Mury." Yet, there was a tradition of 'bunking off' which was probably the same in all big cities. John Milton, the well-known antiseptic poet, might have described the London equivalent of my Liverpool saggers in words akin to those of the following poem:-

18

BUNKER MENTALITY.

As one who oft in populous school-room pent,
Where pellets thick and thicker pupils lay,
At tintinabulation of the bell, once struck,
Proceeding, scorning now the Groves of Academe,
He bunked off out, bent double, stooping low,
Demeanor sly, an all-out 'sagging' gait.

Him later, wrapped in Morpheus' dark arms,
In stygian pit of Odeon, Leicester Square.
With sounds or Orphean or of Loony Toons,
With bugs the Bunny or Cyclops Magoo,
He was espied by one of truants' dread,
Who fused the roles of harpy, fate and snitch,
And bore foul cognomen 'Probation Man.'

Between the Scylla of his outstretched arm,
And the Charybdis of his deft left boot,
Our hero sprung. He fled from noon to night
That Summer's day, and begged for hand-outs
To defray th' expense, til lengthening shadows
On the Waterfront, heralded in birdsong as
Canary Wharf, enveloped him in Phoebus, dying wake.
So back to Mum, a Cockney Pearly Queen,
He fled to beg her to take scrip and write
To Senior Guardian at th' Academy,
That he afflicted was with palsy vile,
Lest, on the morrow, he chastised should be.

See how Arcadia and Arcades corrupt the brain.
Thus ends my hernia, or my epic strain.

A WORD TO THE SAP.

It was G. K. Chesterton who wrote that: "A teacher who is not dogmatic doesn't teach. A teacher who is too dogmatic doesn't educate."

When I first told my father that I was considering becoming a teacher, he paled and said: "How could you bear the responsibility?" I said: "Come off it. You're a doctor. You deal with life and death every day." He replied with unwonted seriousness: "Being a mechanic of the body is difficult, but being a mechanic of the mind and heart and soul must be an awesomely terrifying responsibility." Those words haunted me all the years I was teaching. And they still do. And so they should.

They haunted me especially when I was teaching Religious Studies. I was fascinated by the relationship between language and religion, and frequently prayed: "I thank you Father for hiding the secrets of the Kingdom from the wise and clever and revealing them to mere children." As, for example, when I was teaching about the occasion when Christ said: "Let the one who is without sin, throw the first stone", and my earnest young seekers-after-truth asked: "If His Mother had been there ...?" Or the time when I asked them why, in apostolic times, the shepherds walked in front of their sheep, rather than behind them, and they replied: "Because they went bare-footed!" Traditional language was a 'restricted code' to them. The words: "Holy Ghost", for example, always intimated "Benign Spook". In the same way, nowadays, the words: "In the name of the Father ..." are baffling to those pupils who do not have a traditional father.

Despite the haunting memories, I still cherish the recollection of a class to whom I put the question: "What is the difference between the Pope and me in regard to infallibility?", and a genius replied: "The difference is that the Pope cannot make a mistake. And you don't".

When I told these stories at a recent conference of teachers of religious studies, many of the delegates, bemoaning the problems of language and culture, were in despair, saying: "You can't teach anything dogmatically nowadays".

I suspect that my father would have said: "How about the glory of God, the beauty of Creation and the primacy of Love?" And he would probably have illustrated what he meant with a poem, such as the following metaphysical ballad.

INFLAMING INFIRMITY.

"Why me, Susie, why me? Was the question she asked.
As she sought some relief from the pain.
"You're my sister, and you surely know I've been good.
And I promise I'll be good again."

"Of course you will, Poppet." Her sister replied,
Anxiety masked with a smile.
"You'd better ask Mummy. She knows more than us.
But first you must rest for a while."

"Why me, Mummy, why me?" She asked, much later on.
Her skin an ethereal glow.
"Will I never be seven, like Susie and Tom?
I don't mind, I just want to know."

"Of course you will, Poppet." Her Mother assured,
"And then ten, and twenty, and more.
Now, you ask your Daddy, he never tells fibs,
I think that's him now at the door."

"Why me, Daddy, why me?" The same question again.
Face colourless, skin drawn and grey.
"If you loved me, Daddy, the way I love you,
I'm sure you could take it away."

"We all love you, Poppet." He said with a sigh,
"And if we could take it, we would.
You'd better ask God, he would not hide the truth,
From someone like you, who is good."

"Why me God's? a question I can't ask." She said,
"He answered a long time ago.
When He told me the love I have now, once I'm gone,
Is the sort that will make your loves grow."

"Ah, seeds of love, Poppet," her Maker had said,
"Dead and buried will flower again.
With our Mummies and Daddies, and all those we love,
For ever and ever, Amen."

DAFFYDIVVIES.

I taught in one of the first Comprehensive schools to be opened in England. I was laughingly known as: "Head of English ... as a second language." The school was built for a thousand pupils but had more than twice that number of boys, when I started there. The school motto was 'It 'im Again'. When a visiting speaker came to address the school at morning assembly, the only advice he got from the Head Boy was: "Don't talk too quickly, or they'll all gerrup an start dancin!"

One day, a group of the English Department was gathered in a corridor, being questioned by a posse of visiting HMI's about the difficulties of teaching in so crowded a school. The youngest teacher explained: "My problem is that I just don't know half the boys, even in my own 'house', and there are twelve houses in the school." The Headmaster was passing and overheard. Interrupting, he declaimed: "I know every boy in this school, by name and by sight, Miss. Murphy." With the faintest trace of a smile, she answered: "I'm Miss. Ekins!"

The pupils had a bolshie but creative sense of language. They were always ready to dispute the difference between 'worral' and 'darrel' or to squabble over the plural of 'daddylonglegses'. Asked, in a scripture class to explain the meaning of the word 'begat', they replied, with one voice: "If you can't fight, wear a big 'at!" They hated having to read poetry or plays, but revelled in improvisation and parody. We re-wrote the canon of English classic verse in their familiar scouse patois, from Wirdswirth and Kipling to Pam Eyres and their own Roger McGough.

While there, I did some examinations for the College of Preceptors which entailed assessed classes in a comparable London school. Both the difficulties and the delights of 'playing with words for educational purposes' were the same. Though, of course, the patois was different. The 'Age of the Romantics' for street-wise London teenagers was twelve to sixteen. For them, Kipling connoted cakes, Hamlet, cigars, while Socrates was a world-cup sweeper from Brazil. What they shared linguistically with their Northern counterparts was a love of parody, as exemplified in the following examples from "Norf an Sarf".

A GLIMPSE OF MULTI-COLOURED BLOOMERS.

I wandered, dozy, wid me cart,

Up Brownlow Hill, to take me welt.

When, of a sudden, I seen a tart,

Da ralmost made me eye-balls melt.

"Ee ar den girl. Ay, be my Bird."

Me throat went dry like at the wird.

Wha rother Judy could I take,

In through the ale-house door each night?

Wha rother feller wooden go

All green wid envy at the sight?

Jet white ev hair. Wid orange gob.

Green eye-lids, Cheeks a rosy blob.

More reely sexy she could get,

Dan pictures surfed from off the net.

An as she walked, 'er 'ips were rocken.

Me heart was poundin somethin shocken.

I luked an luked. Oh, warra twit,

It surely learned me, didnit?

For while this judy broke me heart,

Some rotten swine had robbed me cart.

THE LAKE ISLE-OF-DOGS.

I can't get me 'ead rand the poems ev Yeats.
Wiv is bean-rows an wattles an clay.
Cos 'oo wants to listen to linnets an that,
In a B-loud glade day after day?

I aint seen no shepherds arand Shepherd's Bush.
Nor Maidens arand Maida Vale.
While darn at 'the Garden', that's 'Covent' to you,
It's not nectar but cans ev light ale.

Yeats's fairy-tale fables of bucolic plagues,
Wiv satyrs an nymphos an stuff.
Aint nuffink compared to the Chelsea King's Road,
Or the Elephant, when it gets rough.

Us Cockneys use rhyming slang all fru the day,
It's like second nature to us.
You'll earwig it riding the boob or the drain,
Or catching the eighty-two fuss.

But one fing I'll say to be fair to this Yeats
Wiv is rivvum an iambic feets.
Though it gives you the 'ump when you read it alard,
It's better than Kelly or Sheets.

KICKING THE HABIT.

The psycholigist's definition of 'habit' as 'capitalising on pleasurable experience' certainly applies to the time I spent as a postulant and novice, at Nunraw, in Scotland, 'trying my vocation' with the Cistercian monks of the Stricter Observance. (They dislike the name 'Trappist' which falsely implies grim athletic asceticism.)

If the purpose of life is to be happy in the knowledge, love and service of God, then the best thing you can do with it is make that a full-time job. Sadly, I have repeatedly made the arrogant presumption that I should do that on my terms rather than His.

At my clothing with the habit, I was given the religious name of Mary Gregory. All Cistercians take Mary as a middle name, although I never heard my name pronounced. We communicated on essentials in signs, so I was designated by the signs for: 'Big Bishop with the Keys Brother.'

Signs preserved the joyful liberation of silence, though they could cause problems. One day, a large window fell from high above where we were working, and was dropping straight onto my head. Brother Thomas was frantically making the sign for 'Duck' which I thought was intended for Brother Donald (Now the Lord Abbot) until I was flattened. The then Abbot, Dom Columban Mulcahy, looked at my gashed brow and said: "Ah. 'Tis the Almighty crowning you in His own way." In response to my unorthodox sign, which even a non-Cistercian would readily have understood, he rang for an ambulance and gave me a book to read on the way to hospital; a life of Saint Gerard Majella entitled: 'To Heaven Through a Window.' Six months later he advised me that my vocation lay elsewhere. (Without the traditional: 'Super tandem tuum.' or 'On yer bike'.)

On the Saturday morning that I arrived back home, the first words my brothers said to me were: "We've kept your boots and borrowed some kit. You're playing in the second fifteen this afternoon at Orrell."

And there came into my head the words of the Prophet Jeremiah: "Can I not do to you what the potter does? It is the Lord who speaks. Yes, as the clay is in the potter's hand, so you are in mine."

We lost 26-6.

ECUMANIAC.

"One in every four folk is a Buddhist,
That lives on this planet, right now."
Said the Guru, in Lotus position.
Thus milking a pet sacred cow.

Well, my Mum and my Dad are both Catholics.
As I am, I'm happy to say.
So, it's either my sister, Jacinta,
Or my brother, Sogyal Rinpoche.

GET A GRIPE.

"Count to ten," my old Granny would tell me,
"Before you give way to your wrath."
So I'd do it, and get to eleven, and then,
It was Thud! Clout! Bang! Wallop! And Boff!

"Let the sun not go down on your anger,"
She'd say when I started to cry.
But I found that I never could get it to stay,
In its rightful place, up in the sky.

A SURE THINGY.

"The Rational man will proportion belief,"
Is the claim Bertrand Russell once made,
"To the evidence that will support it.
So, I don't have a faith, I'm afraid."

"I fear," said his bookie, in answer,
That's not a belief I can trust.
If you back all the favourites, for ever,
In the long run you're bound to go bust."

AROMA FELIX.

One of my favourite Christian-Zen parable-koans is the tale of the elderly ascetic miracle-working Cistercian monk who was asked the secret of his holy serenity. "For fifty-seven years," he replied, "I have stood next to Brother Gregory in choir, slept next to Brother Gregory in the dormitory, worked next to Brother Gregory in the scriptorium, and even relaxed next to Brother Gregory in the calefactory." Then, after a long pause and a deep sigh: "And Brother Gregory has horrendous B.O."

This story always reminds me of the jibe made by missionaries in the first centuries of the Christian era about the Desert Fathers: "Whose feet do they wash?"

B.O. and un-washed feet are not the only distractions in Church today. They have been joined by unsavoury texts and music of the wrong flavour. Eye-brows, if not objections, were raised recently at my God-Daughter's wedding when she chose the theme from Star Wars as a recessional anthem, though many thousands of Star Wars fans listed their religion at the last census as Jedi. Still, the press has recently carried stories of clergy banning certain tunes and songs from their churches at weddings and funerals. Notably the Blake-Parry setting of Jerusalem. One defender of the idiosyncratic rights and rites of the faithfull improved on an old proverb by claiming that: "He who sings well prays twice, while those around he who sings badly pray three times."

Fragrant elderly Cistercians will know of precedents for Pop in the Pews, if not Motown on the Misericordes. In the Metz Antiphonary there is a marginal gloss on the Allelujah of the mass for the feast of Saint Bernard of Clairvaux, warning that: "Hic est cantus secularis!"

Neither history nor hysteria records whether it ever reached number one in the Carta Caritatis! This is a dreadful joke which would only be understood by elderly Cistercians. The Carta Caritatis is the title of the Charter of Charity, or Love, which was one of the earliest mystical treatises on which the Institutions of the order were based. It was written at the end of the first millennium by Saint Stephen Harding, who was an Englishman. He would doubtless have up-dated Blake's lines to read 'dark Satanic Mills and Boon'. He would probably not have approved of secular songs in sacred settings.

Like that other much neglected great Englishman, Alcuin of York, tutor to Charlemagne, Stephen Harding saw himself as a citizen of Christian Europe; no mean continent. He would not have understood a Eurovision which only extended to Song Contests. As in "Voici le resultat des votes du Church of England Synod: Jerusalem; Nul points!"

The modern English-born American writer and mystic Thomas Merton, long before he became a Catholic, let alone a Cistercian, wrote a master's thesis which was roughly an investigation as to whether William Blake was a genuine mystic or a dirty old man, and concluded that he was both. The extent or quality of his Odor Notus did not feature, and so he passes into hagiographical history as yet another example of morally flawed artistic genius. Like Judas Iscariot, who cured the sick and cast out devils just as effectively as the other eleven. One fierce defender of the cakes-and-ale school of nuptial liturgy, recently bleated in the press that: "Its not as if they were going to sing: 'And did those sweaty feet ...' or 'bring me my B.O. of burning gold ...'"

When I was a novice, we were permitted to speak to the Novice Master on matters of spiritual direction and to the Abbot in emergencies; though it was recommended that this should be on the knees and in Latin, which tended to limit conversation to; "Quid dicis?" "Mea culpa." "Surgite in nomini Domini." And a penance. Any priest could be asked anytime to hear confession and there was access to an 'Extra-ordinary Confessor'.

The most 'extraordinary' confessor I have ever encountered was not in the monastery but back in my native Liverpool.

One evening, I called in to St.Nicholas' Pro-Cathedral on Copperas Hill. There being a light on over the confessional, indicating the presence of a priest, I went in and made my confession. At the end of my recital of an embarrassingly long list of sins, there was a slight shuffle of feet and a low cough, but not a word. Deciding that the priest was elderly and deaf, I repeated my confession more slowly and much louder. This time, after another long silence there was the distinct sound of bucket and mop and a cheery female voice which said "There's no one here, Luv!"

I can't remember what my response was, but I know it was sufficiently forceful to add yet one more to my list of sins.

PABULUM MORTIS: OR KICKING UP A STINK.

I'm cursed with having sweaty feet,
To tread the primrose path,
To Heaven where the angels will
Have run a scented bath.

One day, feet first, I'll surely go,
Into the earth's dark floor.
And hope the stench of my poor feet,
Will fade for evermore.

A martyr to my feet, I've been.
But once I'm cold and stiff,
The incense-laden air will soon
Disperse the slightest whiff.

The medic saints will welcome me.
Saint Luke will be the first.
"Of all I've ever seen," he'll say,
This tinea's the worst."

"A spiritual athlete, me,"
I'll steadfastly maintain,
"This spiritual athlete's foot
My solitary stain."

Then wreathed in clouds of healing balm,
To purgatory I'll go.
To do my time with smelly souls,
Afflicted with B.O.

There Odor-Eater Cherubim,
All redolent of myrrh
Will smother me with frankincense
Like all the in-souls there.

And when my penance is complete,
With feet in scent new shod.
I'll rise refreshed on winged heels,
To take my place near God.

So there! Amen.

HOW WELL DO YOU KNOW ROMAN CATHOLICISM?

Try the following test:-

1. Moses crossed the ... River Jordan: Sea of Reeds: Rubicon: Floor of the House: Sphinx with a Mummy?
2. Martin Luther was a ... Heretic: Charismatic: King: Bath-Sponge: Simpson?
3. Who was chosen as an Apostle ... Bartholomew: Bar Abbas: Bar Sinister: Bar Nabby Rudge: Bar Stool: Bar None?
4. Which of these sayings is in the gospels .. Hold your horses: All shall be well: Whence comest thou: Woe to you Sassenachs: Make my day: It is more blessed to give than to receive?
5. Who was a famous Scribe ... Ben Nevis: Ben Ezra: Ben Edict: Nicky Demus: MacAbeus: Jerry Mire?
6. Which of the following are Roman Colleges ... The Venerable Bede: The Ambrosiana Cream Rite: The Lutheran Basilica: San Francisco: Sant' Anselmo: Santa Fey Trail; San Fey Rien: Trevi Fountain Comp?
7. Who came Fourth ... Adam: Noah: Lazarus: Pope Pius The: Uriah the Heapite: A Flying Eagle?
8. Whose wife, or cucumber, was ... Anna Nyas: Phyllis Tine: Bath Sheila: Tabitha Doormat: Cleopastra: Sapphira?
9. Which of these is an old-fashioned penance ... Seven Sweaty Palms: Limbo Dancing: Strawberry Indulgence: The Stations of Merscyrail: Florentines: Quarantines: Clementines?
10. Which is a legitimate title ... Knight of the Whited Sepulchre: Vicar For Rain: Archipelago Ad Nutum: Mother Exterior: Defensor Vinculi: Brother Canuspareadime?
11. Who is the Senior Cleric ... Mother Hubbard: Archie Bishop: Peter Spence: Sergeant-Major Superior General: Cardinal Sin: The Apooplectic Nuncio: The Doge of Venice?
12. Where would you find together ... Fathers Brown, Malachy and Duddleswell with Monsignor Quixote, Cardinal Consignione and Pope Hadrian?
13. Which of the following is a popular prayer ... De Profundis: Regina Coeli: O Sacred Rota: Ne Temere: En ego: Rerum Novarum: Non Satis Nisi Optimum: Da Mihi Lunam: Quemadmodo iubet? Lilium Candidum.
14. Which of these is a Catholic hymn ... Lord, let this transport last: See the hosts of Hell advancing, Satan at their head: I feel my bowels warmly moved. God likes pie ...ous hearts: Stir that stew...pid soul. Catch that flea...ting moment.

ANSWERS:

1. Yam Suf = Red Sea. Usually translated Sea of Reeds. Perhaps Nile?
2. A charismatic heretic.
3. Nathaniel.
4. None. The last saying appears in an epistle.
5. Ben Ezra. See Chronicles, Nehemiah, etc. With different spelling, Saint Benedict of Nursia, author of the Holy Rule, would qualify.
6. Sant 'Anselmo, the Benedictine Mother House. Venerabile and Beda are runners-up on a spelling technicality. (Runner-uppers?)
7. The flying eagle. Fourth of the four 'animals' at the Throne described in the Apocalypse/Revelation; taken to represent the fourth evangelist since the time of Saint Irenaeus: hence the eagle-book-stand for the gospels in many Anglican churches.
8. Sapphira, wife of Ananias, patrons of married couples? See Acts. 5.
9. Quarantines = periods of forty days: i.e. Lent. Penances were given in years and/or quarantines.
10. Defensor vinculi = defender of chain or: 'Of the bond': an official in marriage tribunals. Vicar Forane = Rural Dean. (Roughly) (But not too!) Ad Nutum = temporary / for the time being / as stop-gap. Not as a newt!
11. Cardinal Jaime Sin of the Phillipines.
12. On a book-shelf. They are fictional clerics in the works of G.K. Chesterton, Bruce Marshall, Neil Boyd, Grahame Greene, Colleen McCullough and Baron Corvo. (O.K. I've never read Thorn Birds so I made up the Cardinal.)
13. En ego. Prayer for thanksgiving after Communion. Attributed to Saint Ignatius Loyola.
One is a psalm, two an antiphon, three a Vatican tribunal, four a decree of that tribunal, six an encyclical, seven Everton Football Club's motto, eight a song by Frankie Vaughan, nine a Roman betting slip, and ten a flower. (Not a prayer but a Madonna Lily.)
14.   All. (Honest.) (Well, nearly all.)

SCORES ON THE DOORS: (Of Saint Peters!) or Rates on the Pearly Gates.
If you got more than half right, then you are an endearing old fogey still in pre-Vat-2 twilight phantom bliss. Less than 50% means that you are what is described in Rome as: "Catolico ma non Fanatico."

URBAN-ITY.

In the city, in my Grandparents' day, they left their houses unlocked. In my parents' day, they left their cars unlocked. In my day, we can't even leave our churches unlocked. Progress it's called. I have fond childhood memories of going on visits, 'down town', to the two-up two-down houses round the courtyards. In every house, the grate was blacked, the brasses were polished and the step was pumiced. And there was a lot of laughter, despite the poverty. They would have enjoyed the tale told recently, by an elderly Liverpudlian, who said: "I grew up in a two-bedroomed house with twelve brothers and sisters. I didn't know what it was like to sleep in a bed all by myself, until I got married!"

It was thirty years and a world war later when television encouraged families to close their doors and turn inwards and offer their children in sacrifice to the fiery idol in the corner. Bingo became the popular escape from house-work though also a drain on the house-keeping purse. The Tally-man's Tin, with its handful of coins, was no longer left just inside the door-on-the-latch for collection. The catalogue and the never-never replaced the All-the-Year-Round clubs and the Penny-in-the-Pound insurance schemes.

Yet another generation was to pass before the electronic age took over, with on-line shopping, e-mail correspondence, and the mobile phone with its shouted pass-word: "I'm on the train". The veneer of political correctness, or 'Lap-top'PC', settled over our cities and the computer illiterate were humiliated with the dreadful curse: "Log Off!"

LOG-OFF LULLABY.

A loud shout of: "I want my Mammon"
Is the cry of this consumer age.
As the children are offered to Moloch.
In the guise of some new IT sage.

Oh, how far are the tropes of this discord,
With its catalogued dim phantom bliss,
From the whispering story at bad-time,
And the blessing that goes with a kiss.

The following two poems are a suggestion as to how Francis Thompson might have shared a house-wife's weekly agony of budgetary juggling, especially in what was: 'Ode to the Rent-Man.' Followed by a cri de curse about the frustrations involved in grappling with what philosophers call the 'ghosts in the machine', or more likely the 'ghouls in the call-centre'.

THE HOUND OF HOUNSLOW

I fled him out the door and cross the yard.
I fled him down the High Street, running hard.
I fled him round the boozer down the square.
And hid from him.

Past many a terraced doorway painted black,
Trelissed with lines of washing, hanging slack.
Dodging the clapped-out motors on the curbs,
And phone-boxes festooned with saucy blurbs,
He followed me. He followed ever after.
As his smelly athlete's feet
Came pounding up the street,
He yelled: "You're six weeks overdue."
I shouted back: "The same to you."
He bellowed, running up the hill,
"I'll catch you soon, you know I will."

But round the corner, out of view,
Into the Bingo Hall I flew.
"Eyes down ... click-click .. the game is on."
The next month's rent is quickly gone.

I know he's waiting at the door,
But, what the heck, just one game more.
I'm bound to win, I thought, some day,
And then the rent I'll gladly pay.

Then it came true - my fondest dream.
The rent-man heard my joyful scream.
And knew at last he'd got no grouse.
He'll get his rent. I've got my 'house'.

34

LÁPRES MIDI D'UN PHONE.

"Welcome to Telecom Madline.
This is Digital Rip-off Com Dot.
Press one if you're calling your Mother.
Push anything else if you're not.

Ring three if you want an alarm call,
or a fireman to rescue your cat.
Try hash, triple three and star zero
 if you're searching for salacious chat.

While the line is on hold,
save, or call-back, you'll hear a concerto or two.
One caller has passed away waiting;
you're now fifty-third in the queue.

We need to confirm who is calling.
State blood group, hat size and address.
To hear a repeat of this message, press,
press press press press press press press.

I'm sorry for that slight confusion:
the lines overload now and then.
If it happens again while I'm speaking:
wait ten minutes then try again.

For death or disaster or flooding,
or a fire that's been raging for long,
We switch you straight to Operations.
And meanwhile we play you a song.

Hello. Fire, Police, Ambulance Service;
give details with chapter and verse.
Press six for a fireman or bobby:
press eight for a doctor or nurse.

For post-trauma Counselling Service:
say 'Yes, thank you' after the tone.
My name's Tricia; have a good day now,
Ooh, there's no need to curse down the phone!"

BEYOND THE PONY-TAIL.

When our girls were away at university, I used to send each of them a weekly letter. They responded with a phone-call to their mother, who would pass on to me the 'edited high-lights' for the following week's epistle.

The letters always contained an old family joke, like: "De disgustibus non est disputandum"; followed by some pastoral guidance, such as: "I have always believed that Saint Paul's advice that 'It is better to marry than to burn with passion' is roughly equivalent to advising someone nervous in the handling of dynamite to get a job in a quarry"; and then an encouraging pious platitude or two, like: "A wise old Novice Master, discussing the calibre of postulants once confided: 'Don't send me fellows who've never been knocked down; send me fellows who know how to keep getting up again.'" Then would come some personal flattery, in the manner of W.S. Gilbert's famous dictum: "You've no idea what a poor opinion I have of myself ... and how little I deserve it." The letters would end with a litany of endearments, warnings and family or neighbourhood gossip.

Of those hundreds of letters, the only ones they still remember are the ones they got the week that I put the letters in the wrong envelopes. They were all up at Oxford at the time, though in four different colleges, and they presumed that I sent the same letter to each of them, copied four times. Consequently, that was the week when 'Chacun a sa Chacune' joined the family cracker-joke repertoire alongside 'Quatorze the Fifteenth'.

Of their many telephone calls, their Mummy now only remembers one. She had never really understood rugby football, and certainly had no idea that University Women's Rugby was quite so popular. So, she dropped the phone and went numb with shock when our youngest confided that she had decided to "become a hooker".

I had to become a 'prop'

BELLE'S LETTRE.

Dearest Daddy, Pater, Pa.
Love to Mummy, Mater, Ma.
Sorry this is rather rushed.
Exams looming, so I'm bushed.
Yes, I know that doesn't rhyme,
But I'm very pushed for thyme.

Got your letter, wrong one though.
SNAFU, blame the G.P.O.
Good news is the resits soon,
Hope to 'sign-on' end of June.
Haven't 'fallen for my Tutor':
Said I'd 'fallen off his scooter'.

There's no sex-change in the air.
Scouts call all the students 'Sir'.
Yes, I've read the Tao of Pooh,
How's that going to get me through?
No, I've not had fights and thumps.
Only rowing and three bumps.

Did get slightly overdrawn.
Nothing left that I can pawn.
(That's a joke for dear Mama.
Wait till she sees my new car.
Bargain from the lad next door.
Twenty quid and worth far more.)

Thinking of a change of course.
New boy-friend's a real dark horse.
Last week we all cried and cried.
Sadie's hamster has just died.
Finals just three days away.
"Snub the grindstone," as you say.

Love and kisses Daddy dear.
Don't believe what else you hear.

WHAT FATE THREW UP.

My earliest gastronomic memories of Liverpool childhood, are of war-time rationing, when the traditional three-course meal was a Dish of Scouse, a plate of Wet Nelly, and a Conny-onny Butty.

When I was away at school in Spinkhill, a diet based on 'Brick and Ditch' resulted in regular outbreaks of what students of culinary West Saxon call Verner's Law of the Great Bowel Shift. This was invariably cured by a visit to the Dispensary, where Matron doled out one, two or three cascara tablets according to the nature and severity of the upset, lesion, deformity or disease. These were ritually fed to her golden retriever on the way out. The pupils throve on this simple pharmaceutical regimen, but the poor dog eventually passed itself quietly away.

Since then, I have had more hot dinners than most people have had hot dinners, but because most of them were the prelude of speech-making I have enjoyed few of them. As a life-long teetotalitarian I dreaded being seated next to a distinguished guest who was a wine fanatic yearning to discuss the cheeky bouquet of the Ugandan Claret. Amateurs should not swop argot with the cognacenti, nor for that matter with the ginenti or the rumenti, I often had to try to recall the post-match bar-room chat of my brothers and team-mates at Sefton Rugby Club, but: "A pint of Drambuie Shandy" somehow never sounded quite right. Once, when my host had sniffed, and swirled the proffered taster of wine, and dismissed the consommeiler with: "Take it away. It's a trifle petulant", I decided to flaunt my hauteur cuisine and rejected my pudding similarly: "Take it away. It's a petulant trifle." A cordon bleu sanitaire descended around me.

It reminded me of the time when we were educational missionaries in Eastern Nigeria. Visiting a village school, we were offered 'chop' containing an unfamilar meat. I enquired: "What kind Beef this be?" The reply was: "Na rabbit." So we tucked in. Later, at another school, we were served 'pot-soup' containing a large water rat. "What do you call this meat?" I asked. The retrospectively disturbing answer was: "Na rabbit."

It was then that we discovered what Napoleon meant when he said that an army marched on its stomach. We also learned why it was that in very rough seas old sea-dogs used to sing "Heave away me hearties..."

NARTHEX NARK

In Old Testament times Sabbath gossips had to be stoned. To hear some parishoners you'd think they already were! As Saint James-the-Less said: 'A bit slipped from a horse's mouth is not as dangerous as a tit-bit from that of a gossip.' Recently, one of the agnoscenti was holding forth in the church porch about 'Declining standards in sacred eloquence...' A passing member of the Sisterhood of Holy Harridans added: "An thir norrasgood at preaching neither!" This unleashed a torrent of 'I remember whens' most of which were so potty, or at least Holy Potty (Fonty?), that I had to praise the great improvements in our Ministry of the Word. This did not appear to make the gaggle of gossips any more gruntled. One of them said: "The Ministry of the Word's not the problem. It's the sermons." I was trying to decide whether this was a non-sequitur, petitio principii or just cobblers, when he added: (For it was a he; the women being conscious no doubt of the Apostle's injunction to say nothing but ask their husbands when they get home.) 'Last week, the priest started out by telling us what the gospel was going to be. Then he read the gospel. Then, for a sermon, he told us what the gospel had been.'
'And what was it?' I asked with provocative gentleness. He glared at me, like a teenager being asked if he was sure he'd finished his homework and then blustered: 'It was er...oh yes...it was about religion...it was that one about pruning the vine. Yes, that's it "I am a vine, and you are the branches".'
"And what," I persisted, "was the message of the homily?"
"We didn't have one of them," he confided, with unctuous injured merit, "but the message of the sermon was: 'Be loyal to the Church. Stick to the true doctrines. Oppose abortion, euthanasia and cloning, otherwise you will be cut off and might end up being burned'." I had been ready to accuse him of confusing the parable with 'the one about the labourers in the brick-yard' but had to admit that there were little nuggets of truth in what he had distilled from the previous week's liturgy. In fact, the only thing he'd missed was the point! The thrice-repeated point that the parable is about 'having life and having it more abundantly'. Maybe the word 'abundantly' threw him? After all, 'The one about abundantly' does not have the sound of authentic familiar simplicity about it. There had been, also, a modern parable illustrating how grafting with vines is done by cutting the wood and joining 'wound to wound', which teaches us compassion for others, since our wounds and theirs are joined by Christ. It was real and profound, not notional and trivial like 'the one about...'
Next week it's 'the one about Zacheus'. It ends with Christ's warning: 'For he too is a son of Abraham'. Like all Christians, all Jews and all Muslims. They share the traditions of the Patriarchs. Abraham who stands for FAITH. Jacob who represents SACRIFICE. And Isaac, which literally means LAUGHTER. And two out of three ain't enough.

SEA SHANDY.

Drink a port in every storm, my lads,
And down your drinks, not tools.
Have a rum in every harbour too.
Britannia waives the rules.

Put some drink in every girl, my lads ,
When she hoists red-in-sign lips.
Try a rum-and-coke and a gin-and-lime.
Then it's down to the she in sips.

Down the hatch with every pint, my lads.
And toast the Plymouth Sound.
Then it's quids pro bono publico.
And double Scotch all round.

These are sad broad thoughts from a home, my lads.
Of nice but nautical days.
Now it's hard'nstern in an invalid chair;
Through a cocoaholic haze

HOARSE SENSE.

Technically, Catholic laymen are only allowed to preach: "By the example of their lives," but I have often been asked to: "Say a few words ... from the pulpit."

I don't know if astro-liturgists use candle-light-years as a unit of measurement, but it sounds appropriate to describe the immense distance which separates pulpits from pews.

Among my clearest memories of school-days are echoes of Jesuits preaching Lenten Sermons about Hell and boys pinning up May Verses about Heaven. I can't recall many Lenten Sermons about Heaven and I have certainly never read a May Verse about Hell.

Nietzsche, the morbid philosopher and nut-case, mostly famous for being spelt wrong, maintained that we only use words which have already died within us. The Christian scriptures proclaim something very different, namely that: "Out of the fullness of the heart, the mouth speaks." In my youth, I sought for the glorious neutral space between these two, where I could metaphorically relax and take off my shoes because it is holy ground. It seemed however to be the rule for preachers in those days that they could beat about any bush as long as it wasn't burning. Pulpit passion was rare. A more usual style of sacred Oratory was typified by the Liverpool Parish Priest known to his peers as 'Parabolam Hank'.

One day, I visited St.Mary's city-centre church to hear an eminent Benedictine monk preach. I was late and sneaked in through a side door, to find myself right beneath the pulpit, at the end of a pew occupied by Mary-Ellens from the local market, many of them wrapped in their black shawls which matched the preacher's cappa magna. As I settled, the monk leaned over the pulpit and announced in ringing tones: "My dears, you've simply got to grasp the ontological imperatives." At which, the Mary-Ellen next to me sighed deeply, gazed up with moist and shining eyes, and announced breathlessly: "Ah, God, isn't he lovely?"

Alas, I was slow to learn the lesson of that exchange. Years later, I began a Lent Address in the neighbouring Anglican Parish Church with the pompous words: "The preacher's aim is to enable the congregation to rise from the simulacra to the subsistent." To which a lady in the front pew responded on behalf of the congregation with a heartfelt: "Ye wha?"

LIKES AND DISLIKES

"Mummy, mummy, mummy…Sister said this morning that Jesus is like us."

"Yes, dear. In everything except sin."

"Well, which of us is He like?"

"All of us, dear."

"Don't be silly, mummy. I'm serious. He can't be like all of us. He wasn't a girl, was He?"

"Well, no dear. He was like all MEN."

"We should say: 'He was like all of THEM.' But He still wasn't: He wasn't married."

"Not all men are married."

"But, not all men are not married, either. He didn't have children, so He wasn't like you and Daddy, for a start."

"But He was a child, and did everything His parents told Him."

"He wasn't a proper child. When He went to the doctors, He ran away. And He talked like a grown-up. I don't think His Mummy would let Him have a dog or a hamster, so He was like me, alright."

"He was God, even when He was a child…"

"A BOY! Then a MAN! He was like never a girl, or a lady, and there is not 'God the Mother' is there?"

"No, dear. I mean, yes dear. He was like all MANKIND. You remember that Sister told a joke about 'Man embraces Woman'?"

"Please, mummy, Daddy promised no more sex education until I do grade five violin. How can Jesus be like us when He didn't have to do piano OR violin? And He had no mobile phone, and no computer, no smelly bus to go to school on, no microwave to feed the five million, no…"

"There weren't any of those things in the first century, two thousand years ago."

"So, we should say that He was like THEM in SOME things, THEN?"

"In all important things."

"Ah, but when we visit Grandma, you say that old people are important, and Jesus never got old."

"No, dear, but He did visit his Grandma. Her name was Anna."

"Was she His mummy's mummy or His daddy's mummy?"

"She was Our Lady's mummy. Saint Joseph was his foster-father. Jesus's real Father was in Heaven."

"That doesn't really sound like us in all things, does it?"

"That's not an important thing."

"It sounds pretty important to me. And I bet it did to Him as well."

"Well, yes, but not as important to us, in making us know Him and love Him, so that we will get to Heaven where his Father is."

"I think that what Sister meant was that: 'He LIKES us in all things'. Then we would love Him and go to Heaven."

"True, dear. He LOVES us in all things except sin…"

"Sister says that He loves sinners especially."

"Sinners, yes, because they are important people, but not their sins which harm everyone and make them unhappy."

"Sister said that Jesus 'Carries all our sins'. Does that make Him unhappy?"

"That's enough for now missy-madam, you ask your Father when he gets home."

"I bet Our Lady never said that to HIM."

LOOPING THE T-LOOP

The microphone clearly redundant,
The preacher's voice louder than loud,
Was telling of voices from heaven,
And God booming out of a cloud.

"These words have come from time immoral."
At least I think that's what he said.
Though 'mists of iniquity' darkly,
Were swirling around in my head.

From a lost 'pre-hysterical era'
Came earache of more recent date.
"Let go of the past", he was urging;
But all we were passed was the plate.

He gave us the sort of a message
That sinners came yards just to hear.
Well, not really much of a message.
More, a tinnitus-buzz in the ear.

At last he switched off the loud speakers,
And gently said: "Now, let us pray.
Let us all say the great prairie tortoise."
So we did, and then all slunk away.

43

MOTHERHOOD.

The Anglican Parish Church of Liverpool, which overlooks the Pier Head, is dedicated to Our Lady and Saint Nicholas.

It is the only Church in England which still continues the tradition, which dates back for more than a century, of having a separate speaker giving a lunch-time address on every week-day of Lent.

I have had the pleasure and privilege of giving one of these addresses each Lent for more than thirty years.

Most of the pleasure comes from attending the services on as many days as possible to hear the word of God proclaimed by a great variety of men and women, clerical and lay, from home and abroad; individually interpreting a common theme of significant relevance to the Easter People of Merseyside.

For a professional speaker, preaching poses a particular problem. The challenge to a presenter or raconteur is to assess the mood and feel of the event, catch the attention of the audience, work on their thoughts and emotions, and leave them stimulated, amused, curious or aroused.

The task for a preacher is to plug the congregation in to the Holy Spirit and then get out of the way! The better he is at the former, the more difficult is the latter.

It is no use looking for a miraculous feed-back of five thousand, but an attentive ear to the critical comments of a few of the congregation, either during or after the sermon, has helped me over the years.

One year, my address contained even more Mariolatry than usual. Afterwards, one of the Anglican Vicars commented: "Like all Roman Catholics, you pay too much attention to sin, and give too much honour to the Virgin Mary." To which I replied that the former is very likely but the latter is quite impossible. To which his riposte was: "There you are, typical!" Which gave me the chance to tell him the following 'typical' Roman Catholic sermon story:

At the last Judgement, the Lord will turn to those Catholics on his left-hand side, and say to them: "I was hungry and you didn't feed Me. I was thirsty and you gave Me nothing to drink. I was sick or imprisoned and you didn't visit Me. I was naked and you gave Me no clothes." And they will reply: "Yes, Lord. It's true, but I am a friend of your Mother's."

All those who appreciate that parable, will understand the following poem:

VISITATION.

I battle with demons of anger and lust,
Whenever I travel by car.
So I space out the journey with psalms or with prayers.
Or the rosary when I go far.

It's all fifteen decades from home to Skegness,
And five more from there back to York.
It's one up to Southport, with time in between,
To engage the Almighty in talk.

I talk to Our Lady, if traffic allows.
She never distracts with replies.
But subtly suggests the right decade to pray,
And sometimes that's quite a surprise.

Once, just going local, I thought I'd no time,
For more than an Ave or two.
But Mary said gently: "Third Joyful today,
A feast very special for you."

It wasn't near Christmas so I asked her why
And softly she answered: "Because,
Today is the day that your Mother was born."
And would you believe it, it was.

Since I had forgotten, it came as a shock.
And taught me a lesson sublime.
The journeys we make in our hearts and our souls,
Extend way beyond space and time.

STAND BY YOUR BEDS.

Most men of my generation did National Service in the armed forces. Some wrote books about it, like David Walder's 'Bags of Swank' or David Lodge's 'Ginger You're Barmy'. All have vivid memories of a unique culture and the esoteric language that went with it.

Many of the cathartic jokes were passed on from unit to unit, and intake to intake, so that even today ex-servicemen gain delight from merely repeating the punch-lines, which go with a vast variety of versions of the parade-ground gag:
'We were, Sarnt-Major, but we didn't like their place of worship.'
'Lucky beggar nuthin, that was me knife, fork an spoon.'
'Hearing the chink of the coin ev the realm, I placed 'im on the report'

My own National Service, delayed by university and monastery, began in a Liverpool Recruitment Office in a bizarre conversation with a crimson-sashed, spit-and-polished Colour-Seargeant: "What do you want, son?"
"I want to do my National Service."
"First lesson, son, nobody WANTS to do his National Service. Anyway, where have you been until now?"
"I've been a monk."
Some colourful Saxon expletives were followed by a long pause, and then: "Can you cook?"

Shortly afterwards, I was called up to the Royal Army Dental Corps. (Excused boots.) After six weeks of basic training, I went via the rugby field, the boxing ring and WOSB to Eaton Hall, where I was a uniquely erkish sprog Officer-Cadet from the Dental Corps. Whence, after briefly joining my 'green-line regiment' which was the King's Liverpool, I went to the Parachute Brigade's famous 'P Company' and was duly commissioned into 2 Para.

From there I went for jump training to RAF Abingdon, where I had to learn a new language. "Right-o chaps. Look in. I'll put you in the picture. You can run it up the balloon cable. Then we'll play it orf of the cuff." i.e. "Hello".

I spent a further two years between Hampshire and the Middle East. My memories are the usual mix of patriotism, service, fun, challenge, and hardship, plus the obligatory favourite army joke and a treasured personal anecdote, of the sort that Rudyard Kipling might have written into his 'Barrack-room Ballads'

BARRACK-ROOM BAD LADS.

"Stand still by your beds. That means perfectly still.
Backs upright. Feet outright. An don't look at me.
If the Officer questions you, look straight ahead.
Come smart to attention, an give your last three.

Barrack shun! As you were! Barrack, wait for it, shun.
Stick Orderly stand by. The rest of you freeze.
O holy Saint Vitus, stop swaying about,
Like great pregnant windmills or forests of trees.

Shift that pack. Bull that brass. Only breathe when you're told.
Get that beret on straight. Yes, you Smith two five nine.
You aint in an outfit of crap-hats an sprogs,
So make sure you've got all those mess-tins in line.

Square off them olive drab greens on that bed,
An don't leave that scabbard all squiffy.
An you, dozy pillock, down there at the end,
It looks like you're one housewife diffy.

All present an waitin inspection, now, Sir.
Less two men in sick-bay, both skiving.
One AWOL, two jankers, four guard-duty, Sar.
And one with the C.O. out driving."

"Right, stand easy, Corporal. Make that man show boots.
If they're diffy on kit they must 'borrow'.
Dirty flesh, muddy floor, idle knife, fork and spoon.
Get it right for the same time tomorrow!"

STAND IN THE DOOR.

My favourite army joke is one which perfectly encapsulates the tri-partite culture-clash of the barrack square. It tells how a weary troop of squaddies were trudging round the square, saluting by numbers, when a doom-laden voice, with touching pathos, moaned: "O death where is thy sting?" The immediate response from an apoplectic drill-corporal was: "OO said that! Come on, Oo said that?" An even wearier voice responded: "No idea, Corporal, but I think it was Shelley." Next day on Part-One Orders was the announcement: "Private Shelley to Adjutant's Office. On report. Insubordination. Twenty-one hundred hours."

My favourite personal anecdote is an example of how a 'laughing AT' joke can give rise to a far more satisfying 'laughing WITH' story.

The original joke was that on the passing-out Queen's Parade at Sandhurst, when her Majesty took the salute, and King Hussein of Jordan was one of the passing-out cadets, there was a moment of profound silence broken only by the stentorian tones of R.S.M. Lord bellowing the immortal words: "Standstill, you idle little Monarch!"

The true follow-on story is that in 1958 we were stationed at Aqaba and some of us were invited to a 'mensive' or 'posh-scoff' in Amman hosted by King Hussein. I asked him if the Sandhurst joke was true. Beaming, he replied: "Oh yes, it is perfectly true. And do you know, the Queen never flinched!" For good measure he then acted-out a parade-ground encounter with R.S.M. Desmond Lynch of the Irish Guards, who had growled in his ear: "If you do not get a grip of yourself, Mr. King, Sir, we will have to report you to your people!"

It wasn't all i/c DTL's on rocky ground!

And some memories never fade. Like that of the RAF Despatcher giving final instructions: "Before you jump, ook up! If your main chute doesn't open, pull your reserve! If your reserve doesn't open, cross your legs left over right, cos it's easier to screw you out on a left-hand thread!"

Followed, on arrival over the D.Z. by: "Red on: stand in the door. Green on: GO!" And then a desperate, faltering, plaintive wail: "As you were!"

~∞∞∞~

SPIT' N' POLISH.

To bull your boots to brightest sheen
Use elbow grease and spittle.
Cos if you want to make them shine,
I promise you that it'll.

~∞∞∞~

ROYAL ARMY DENTAL CORPS BLIMEY.

Looking down in the mouth is a dentist's sad fate.
Even when he has suave charm and wit.
The punch-line to all his best stories remains:
"Now please rinse your mouth out, and spit."

Hanging up on the wall, in a BDA frame,
Is a hymn called 'Abideth with Me.'
It says 'Change and decay' (Rampant mouth-rot to you.)
'Is all around'. (As you can see.)

He asks searching questions, while poking about
With padding to keep your gums dry.
"No smoking," he cautions, "and mind what you chew."
Ignoring your strangled reply.

To the Vestal Accomplice who stands at his side,
In a code which it seems never varies,
He says: "Eight, seven, filling, gap, persistent E,
    Upper wisdom, gap, occlusal caries."

When he's crossed your last bridge, and it's safe to respond,

And you're too numb for any more spitting.
Suggest that the sign on the door should be changed:
    "A chipped yellow plaque would be fitting."

DUMBING UP.

When I was lecturing to Polytechnic Students, some of whom sometimes regarded themselves as failed University Undergraduates, I used to boost their self-esteem by telling them about the Mediaeval Dominican friar, Thomas Aquinas, Patron Saint of students, father of scholasticism, and writer of the first Limerick. Though he was one of the greatest intellectuals ever born, he was regarded by many of his contemporaries as 'thick' because he was 'thick-set'. Indeed his nick-name in his student days was 'The Dumb Ox'. The incident in his life which under-achieving students always warmed to, concerned the occasion when his Professor, and fellow Dominican Friar, Albert the Great, was lecturing in a theology seminar and was advised by the students that he would not get any sense out of 'the Dumb Ox.' He replied, and I paraphrase, but accurately: "When the names and works of all of you lot have long been forgotten, the bellowings of this 'Dumb Ox' will still be echoing around the world." As indeed they are.

Sadly, his first Limerick is not heard very often nowadays since the Roman Catholic Church has moved away from Latin to vernacular liturgies. Thomas Aquinas was a poet as well as a theologian, and wrote some of the greatest Latin Hymns ever used in the Church, such as the Lauda Sion, verses of which are still sung at eucharistic liturgies all over the Christian world.

That proto-Limerick is in fact part of a eucharistic prayer, which all Roman Missals used to print as a Thanksgiving After Holy Communion. The relevant lines, make a beautiful prayer in themselves:

> Sit vitiorum meorum evacuatio,
> Concupicentiae et libidinis exterminatio.
> Caritatis et patientiae,
> Humilitatis et obedientiae,
> Omniumque virtutum augmentatio.

Readers whose Latin scholarship now consists of vestigial aphorism like 'Amo, Amas, Amatitagain', will doubtless now be muttering to themselves such imprecations as:
"Quemadmodo, tunc, hunc, nunc?" or "Howsabout that, then, now?" and demanding a translation of Thomas of Aquino's Limerick. Thus:-

> May it make all my vices decrease.
> And my greed and my lust wholly cease.
> But make humble love grow,
> By the Spirit's warm glow,
> In obedient patience and peace.

Translation never does full justice to the original, especially when the original is a Limerick. Even variant vernaculars of English can be baffling at times, as I discovered with a Limerick I wrote in Scouse many years ago:

> A Scouser lass known as R-Mury
> Sold goose-gogs outside ev the Dury.
> I asked: "Wharar thee wack?"
> "I dunno," she said back.
> "Thir like gear little plums ony ury."

I recited this one day to some friends from Manchester, and one of them asked me to "lern 'im it." Years later, I asked him to recite it for me, and he obliged:

> A lass down ar lane 'oos name't Mary,
> Saw a goosebry one day intut dairy.
> An she said: "Ee bah gum.
> It looks jus like a plum,
> Burrits got lickel wings like a fairy."

Some years later, again, I recited both versions in a debate at the Oxford Union and asked anyone who felt inclined to re-translate the Limerick into accepted standard Oxford English. As I sat down the President handed me a piece of paper on which was inscribed:

> A Merseyside maiden, Maria,
> Dispensed fruit to each casual buyer,
> She passed-off to her chums,
> As fine hirsute plums.
> What were in fact specimens of the sub-species:
> Ribes Grossularia.

For those who did not have the benefit of Greats, it means 'Goose-gogs'.

If the Dumb Ox was writing verses for Oxbridge today, they might be like this:

> "Infinity approximates to Zero,"
> The Prof. Claimed: "It's simple, you see."
> "It may be to you," said his student,
> "But it means 'Next to Nothing' to me."

Had the Angelic Doctor lived in England rather than Italy, he would probably have had to adopt a style like that of William Blake:

> A troop of monkeys in a zoo,
> Puts all heaven in a stew.
> Even as they ask each other:
> "Am I truly my keeper's brother?"

The great logician might have up-dated the fallacy of undistributed muddle:

> A Philosopher Landlord, increasing the rent,
> Destroyed all his tenants' illusions
> Claiming: "All rules of logic support my intent,
> My premisses force my conclusions."

The saintly friar, who wrote in the Nicomachean Ethics that: "Unmitigated seriousness betokens a lack of virtue, since it does not allow due time and space for rest and play", might even have written, playfully:

> "So crates of beer let them bring in!"
> The pupil actor cried with joy.
> His Master shouted from the wings:
> "It's Socrates bier, you stupid boy.",

FRANGLAIS.

For lovers of the arcane niceties of spoken English, Modern Language Departments provide the best fun. I remember from my own schooldays a Polish teacher shouting in frustration: "You think I know damm nothing. I tell you I know damm all!" ·

Students of German tend to be pedantic. Like the one whose computer was not working and reported that it was 'on the dole'. French students are more imaginative, as with the translation of 'Le coeur a ses raisons' as 'The choir has got grapes', or even 'Moi aussi' as 'I come from Sydney'.

My favourite story, however, is of the English teacher meeting a party of exchange French students at Victoria Station. He arrived late and found that they had all gone down into the Underground. Dashing down the stairs, he found the first of them in tears, moaning: "I do not have any dog", and pointing to a sign which warned: "Dogs must be carried on the escalator." Half-way down the platform, he found another pupil standing stiffly to attention, who announced proudly: "I am 'minding the gap'". At the end of the platform, he finally caught up with the French teacher and asked her if she had had a good crossing on the Channel Ferry. "No," she replied, "La Manche was very rough and in my cabin I had the bottom bunk. In the bunk above me was an English boy who was very sea-sick and who kept shouting: 'Look out!' when he meant: 'Look in!'"

In these days of political correctness most linguistic jokes are ruled out, but I still enjoy the tale of the Swedish visitor who thanked his hostess, at the end of his visit, with the words: "I hope I have not cockroached on your hospitality?" "No," she corrected him, gently, "you should say 'encroached' not 'cockroached'". "Ah, yes, of course," he said, "I was forgetting that you are a woman."

For a corrective to this sexism, there is the story of the Englishman and Frenchman chatting when a fly landed on a mirror at the far end of the room. "Voila," said the Englishman, "regardez le mouche." "Non, non," said the Frenchman, "c'est LA mouche." "Hell's teeth," said the Englishman, "you must have fantastic eye-sight!"

POMMES DE FRANGLETERRE.

"Give us five parnds ev spuds," the youth asked of the man
Who kept the stall down the Arcade.
"That's five parnd ev spuds," he repeated himself.
"And two pints of white lemonade."

"Don't they teach you no weights or no measures, an that?"
The green-grocer said, with disdain.
Now it's all grammes an litres. It's gone metric like.
The same as in France, or in Spain.

"Right then," the lad countered, with nonchalant air,
"Give us five parnds of grammes, mon bon man.
An two pints of litres, in one large pouvoir.
That's French. An it means 'In a can'"

****

FAUX PAS DE DEUX

"Que je suis fatigué," the French visitor sighed,
As he slumped down upon the setee.
"Je suis tres fatigué.
Do you know what it means to be 'tres fatigué mon amie?"

"It means that you're stout, or you're chubby at least,"
His hostess replied with some glee.
"But your sexual orientation remains
A well-guarded secret with me!"

UNCONSCIOUS NINE-IRONY.

When we stopped playing rugby, my brothers all started playing golf, which I resisted so effectively that to this day I don't even know the elementary rules, such as how many bats you are allowed to carry in your case.

My antipathy dates from the occasion of the very first invitation to a family golf day which I declined in order to play one last game of rugby. I was well past my scrum-by date and should have known better, but it was an evening game at Birkenhead Park, over on the other side of the Mersey and several regulars were not available.

"You can stand around at full-back," the Captain assured me, "and stroll about, enjoying the evening air."

Half-way through the second half, the opposition hooker launched a towering 'Garryowen'. I watched it carefully and shouted loud and clear: "Yours!" but nobody took any notice and they all hit me.

I woke up several days later, back on the Liverpool side of the river, in bed in a side-ward of a neurological section of Walton Hospital.

As I regained consciousness, a doctor started flashing a torch in my eyes and asking daft questions about how many fingers he had and what was the date and did I remember getting into the hot bath after the game last Wednesday?

I didn't. In fact I remembered nothing after the up-and-under. With them up and me under.

Eventually, the doctor gestured behind him and said: "Your wife is very worried." Sitting in the far corner of the room was my wife, looking very worried indeed.

I smiled at her re-assuringly and she put down her magazine and approached my bed. Bending low over me, her eyes moist and her brow furrowed, she murmured very slowly and deliberately, the encouraging words: "Where the hell's the car?"

PSEUD FOR DAMAGES.

****

Send out the fraud squad.
Grab the swindlers quick.
The C.I.D. are keen to get
Their twisters in a nick.

****

Hebrew script runs right to left.
Which makes it hard for me.
If English writing was the same.
Be would it awkward how.

****

By standing on his dignity, he squashed it.
Gaining stomach when they said he would lose face.
Then he made it worse by resting on his laurels.
Which meant he wore them in a funny place.

****

"What makes people tick, tis my duty to probe,"
The Irish psychiatrist said to his brothers.
"The problem for us," they replied, "is to guess,
What makes you much ticker than others."

STAGES OF EVILUTION.

Communication is a mechanism for bridging distances. Man's first great evolutionary leap is supposed to have been developing the ability to speak. I think it was developing the ability to throw. Lots of animals give mating calls and warning cries, but only man defeats his adversaries at a distance by using his arms to throw weapons.

The second great advance of homo communicans is supposed to have been the development of writing. That way you can send messages down the ages. The ultimate triumph of writing came with printing, when all the gurus proclaimed that you no longer have to be old to be wise. Reading one book a week, any man can, in one year, acquire the wisdom of the fifty greatest men who ever lived. And so, the first books to be printed in English were the Bible, Thomas a Kempis' The Imitation of Christ, Abelard's Sic et Non, and Chaucer's Canterbury Tales. Lo and behold, in only half a millennium we reached page three of the Sun.

The next discovery, which made us once sound-bitten twice sound-shy, was radio communication which girdled the earth in seconds. And who was the most influential broadcaster of the twentieth century: Joseph Goebels.

Which brings us right up to the computer age and the ultimate contradiction: 'virtual reality'. There are now billionaires peddling 'solutions' for which other billionaires have to work day and night in order to create the problems.

No wonder we are now told that: "Your communicative power will largely depend on how well you are able to 'boot your systems'."

I'll stick with chucking, like my ancestors.

IAMBIC PARKINGMETER.

Horn-hogging madman. Red and sweaty face.
Late for appointment. Needs to grab a space.
Daren't risk a clamping. Had too many fines.
Nothing in sight but double yellow lines.
Anger and panic. Leave it on the verge?
Stop at a hotel, tip the concierge?
Some one just leaving? Go round one more time?
Feeding the meter! Surely that's a crime?
Woman reversing makes a gap at last.
Then stalls it side-ways, nothing can get past.

No football icon, when deprived of drink.
No game-show hostess, being forced to think.
No euro-sceptics served with Brussels sprouts.
No punch-drunk boxer, after fifty bouts.
No seedy pop-star when weaned off the dope.
No clapped-out actress killed-off in a soap.
No I.T. hacker whose P.C's gone down.
No country bumpkin forced to live in town.
None felt such anger, road-rage or despair.
As that poor driver, tearing out his hair.

Finally tucked in, neatly on the kerb.
Euphoriarising, if that is a verb.
Now for the meeting. Really have to dash.
Feels in his pocket. Finds he has no cash.
Curses the meter, and the Warden too.
Just when you need one, there's not one in view.
Sees that the coin slot's covered up with rust.
Sticks a note on it: 'This machine is bust.'
No second thoughts now, nor a second glance.
Might get a ticket, have to take a chance.

Meeting soon over. No time for a jar.
Finds there's a warden writing by his car.
Mind still in turmoil, trying to unwind.
Says: "You can stick it ..." then changes his mind.
"This machine's broken. Tried my level best."
"Sir is a comic. What a merry jest."
Street soon resounding with the driver's shout:
"I'll give you jest, you gibbering great lout.
Fat, ugly monkey! Drivelling poltroon!
Vile spawn of Satan! Arrogant baboon!"

Warden smiling answers: "Sir should be discreet."
As men in white coats drag him up the street.

GOGGLE-BOXING

In the seventies and eighties I did a great deal of week-end radio and television broadcasting: religious slots for Anglia and Grampian, chat-shows for ABC and Ulster, magazine programmes for Tyne-Tees and Thames, quizzes for ABC and BBC. I prefer radio to television. A Shakespeare tragedy on radio is a feast for the imagination. On television the pictures keep getting in the way.

I took some panning from the critics over the years, but the most significant criticisms came from my pupils. I still fondly recall the opening dialogue to an English class, first thing one Monday morning:
"I seen you last night. You was bum."
"No, lad I SAW you last night and you WERE bum."
"Well, you was, an all."
"Look, I never want to hear you say 'seen' again, always 'saw'. Now back to Hamlet. Where are we up to?"
"Act four, saw three."

Ironically, it was a Granda Television series on After-Dinner Speakers called 'My Lords, Ladies and Gentlemen' that persuaded me to switch from broadcasting to conference speeches and presentations.

I soon learned to appreciate stories like the one about the gorgeous blonde who sidled up to a staid businessman guest at the conference pre-dinner reception and announced in a loud voice: "I've slept with you." "No, no" he protested feebly, "mistaken identity. When was this anyway?" "During the first presentation after lunch."

My favourite conference story came from a sermon by that great Liverpudlian Passionist evangelical, Father Austin Smith. Thus: "At the Last Judgement, the Lord will turn to those on His left-hand side, and He will say to them ... 'Right, I want you all to break up into small discussion groups ... and report back after purgatory.'"

As a Vicar said to the Television Producer at the Wedding ceremony: "I would prefer it if you would say 'I do'  rather than 'I'll buy that. So it's a wrap.'"

SONGS FROM THE SOUR-GRAPE-VINE.

****

On a plaque on the wall of a posh London House.
In an envied sought-after position.
It says: "Burne-Jones the Painter lived here for some years."
It's now in a dreadful condition.

****

From four storeys up in the tenement block,
The voice choed down in the yard:
"If you're not wearing knickers get in here at once.
Do you hear me, now, Scheherezade!"

****

My wife's PC outlook will brook no dissent,
Or chauvinist comments from me.
I dare not be ageist or sexist with her.
She's post people-o-pausal you see.

****

"From when you were AC2/Stores at Brize Norton,
You owe two million pounds," the Air Ministry wrote.
"For mistaking 'Ten hangars/Large Size/Airoplane',
For 'Ten Hangers/Clothes/Overcoat'."

WRITER'S CAMP.

After a meeting of the 'Press Gang' in Fleet Street, a notice appeared in a newsletter which claimed that: "At the start of the meeting, our Guest Speaker was applauded in, and at the end he was clapped-out."

The 'Press Gang' represents the technical, production, engineering side of the printing industry. The journalistic side is represented by the Newspaper Society. At their conferences, alongside much hard work, there is often a fun competition with a prize to be added to the awards presentations. I have fond memories of a Limerick contest, a Spoof Classified competition, and a Mock Headline contest. The closest I ever came to winning was with this poem based on the motto of Fleet Street:

> "The pen is mightier than the sword," they say.
> And ink is far cheaper than blood.
> So it's: "Fix nibs and charge at the enemy, men.
> And drown them with Quink in a flood.
> With Platignum Corps standing firm to the rear;
> And Biro Platoon on the flanks.
> Let's load-up on ball-points, with blotters unfurled;
> And then we can write-off their tanks."

My efforts at writing spoof headlines were even less successful. I never managed to come up with anything that would rival:-

MAN HIT BY BUS CRITICAL.

I'd be blazing abusive, myself!
Many editors claim a version of the announcement which I first heard ascribed to a Lancashire Daily, after the sinking of the Titanic:-

WEST-HOUGHTON LAD FEARED DROWNED.

This is what journalists call; "Putting a nose on a piece". It serves to remind readers that communication that does not lead to community is sterile. It also helps to remind religious journalists that community that does not lead to communion is pagan. And when I was writing both religious and secular articles it constantly re-assured me that communicaction and ex-communication are not incompatible.

FREUDIAN SLIPPAGE.

Behavioural psychology is where you throw a laboratory rat on the fire and shout: "Jump off." At the end of a week, it will jump off without you having to say a word. It has therefore: 'learned a new behaviour.'

I once asked a student what he had learned from the salivating of Pavlov's dogs and he replied that he had learned not to back them until he had seen them race three or four times.

If you think that is a terrible joke, then you have forgotten that Sigmund Freud's study of jokes had the catchy, give-away title: "The Psycho-pathology of Everyday Life." Even his informative joke about the: "Man from Fulda, training the perfect horse ..." which he tacked onto the end of the fourth of his U.S. lectures on psycho-analysis is now only remembered in garbled sniggers about: "Getting your oats." For Freud's German contemporaries, the phrase: "There was this man from Fulda ..." signalled a joke. Like the Polak joke in the U.S.A. Or the Neufy joke in Canada. Or the Van de Merve joke in South Africa. Or the Kerryman joke in Ireland. As in: "Did you hear about the Kerryman who took his car in for its first service, and crashed it into the pulpit?"

It was almost, but not quite, a psychiatrist's joke, when Jung said that Freud: "Went down deeper, stayed down longer, and came up dirtier than anybody else." And it was almost, though not quite, a Zen joke, when the Dalai Lama said that psycho-analysis is like stirring up a nest of hibernating snakes, removing the most poisonous ones, and leaving the rest to come out when the weather warms up.

My favourite 'psychiatric one-liner' comes from the Liberal Rabbi, Lionel Blue. He tells of the occasion when a student burst into his office shouting that he was going to commit suicide and demanding: "What are you going to do about it, Rabbi?" In describing his response, the Rabbi uses a sentence which out-freud's Freud: "For the next half-an-hour or so we practised jumping off the sofa."

Now that's behavioural psychology!

OEDIPUS-IN-BOOTS.

Little Polly Crates, overcome with grief,
Looks for Annal Gesic, seeking pain relief.
Achilles, in his armour, just come back from Crete,
Buys elastic stockings, martyr to his feet.
Bossy Aggie Memnon, should have been a boy,
Rows with Minnie Laus, setting off for Troy.
Wise old Harry Stottle, looks for Philosan.
Or some Grecian fillip, in a tube or can.
Aged seer Thermosthenes buys himself a flask.
Wanted thermal long-johns but too shy to ask.
Pat Moss looks for Ajax, got a floor to mop.
Needs to go to Argos, that's a bigger shop.
By the pet-food counter, a Dalmatian with his pup.
Not true Greek but Attic, comes from higher up.
Archie Medes bath-salts cost a lot of money.
Old Harry Stophanes, thinks that's very funny.
Narcissus tries his mobile, Perse-phone's engaged.
Pteflon has to stick to Pan's, Medea is enraged.
Di Ogones and Taphius, Bachae up from Wales,
Hunt for Zephyr's wind pills, going in the sales.
Over in the corner, Hysteria not far,
The Pantheon of Pantyhose, shields nervous Hygeia
Trying tinted lenses, Niobe all tears.
Mascara, running swiftly, hides her darkest fears.
Echo buys a hearing aid, a mirror and a comb.
Didymus the twin arrives and Solon on his own
Procrustes wants a bed-pan. Mustn't be too small.
Icarus needs sun-block, to try and break his fall.

Whatever Freud and Jung might say,
In life there's little new.
For all our fads and foibles, well,
The Greeks had a word for it too.

64

SPENDING TIME.

Many stories are told about the comedian, Ken Dodd, the Squire of Knotty Ash. Here are two. The first is probably apocryphal. The second is certainly true.

The first relates to the famous trial: 'Dodd versus the Inland Revenue', the bizarre high-point of which came when Roy Hudd, who was a character witness, told the jury how generous Doddy is: "When he's on stage, you can't get him off. When he makes a speech, he always over-runs. He is supremely generous with the precious gift of his time." At which the Defence Counsel turned to his Junior and announced in a loud voice: "My great fear is that if he gives him five years, he'll do seven."

The true story concerns a Charity Bingo Hall that used to operate in Birkenhead. When they had built up a sizeable kitty, they would invite a representative of a nominated charity to bring a celebrity guest to perform at a gala night and receive a cheque. One evening, I went as a guest with a Sister of the Medical Missionaries of Mary, to accept a donation for their missionary work in Nigeria, where my wife, Noelene, and I had worked with them in the sixties, and where our first daughter, Catherine, was born. The Principal Guest was Doddy, who brought with him a fund-raiser from the Clatterbridge Hospital on the Wirral to receive the donation.

On arrival we were ushered into the upstairs VIP Suite, which consisted of a large lounge and seating area, with a bar and a small stage, on which, as we arrived, a mature, local aspiring comedian was performing. Actually, he was 'dying', while the members totally ignored him, as they stood around chatting and drinking.

Doddy took this all in at a glance, carried his chair up near to the stage, laughed, clapped and showed every sign of enjoying the comic's desperately feeble routine. The focus and the mood of the room changed. At the end of the 'turn', Ken Dodd led the applause and then unobtrusively took the performer aside and said: "Here's a couple of gags you might like to use in future ..."

Ever since that day, I have been determined that if I was ever asked to do five years for Doddy, I'd gladly do seven.

He is one of the people who convinces me of the truth of the line from the Koran which says: "He deserves Paradise who makes his companions laugh."
Kenneth Dodd fits well into that long line of companionable English laughter-makers which stretches back to Geoffrey Chaucer.

Had they been contemporaries, Chaucer might well have immortalised him thus:-

DODDY THE MARMALISER.

A Diddy-man with us ther was also,
That far from Knotty Ash had long y-go.
His teethe gleamed in his head aright.
As doon chip butties on a frosty night.
His tickling stick he bar ful like a lance.
For he could of that art the olde dance.
His word was: "Ee ar Missus," moot I thee,
Full loud he song of "'appiness" to me.
At th'equinoxial in the month of May,
To finals of the cups he went alway.
I saw, Lordyngs, full sheen upon his car,
The motto 'Anfield Vincit Omnia.'
Great tufts of hair grew from his skulle bones.
A Scally-Wacker was he for the nones.
Snuff mines and sarny works was al his play.
"Tattifilarious" - there is namore to say!

canteR Butty tale

"I went to Canterbury, missus, and all I got was this lousy tabard."

WE LEAVE NO TURN UNSTONED.

One evening, some years ago, I arrived at the home of Wigan Rugby League Football Club to speak at a Sportsmen's Dinner.

Northern hospitality is legendary, or as they say in Wigan 'Without peer', but I was somewhat taken aback to find that I was listed on the menu as: 'Number Three Turn'. I sought clarification from the Social Secretary who was, as they as thereabouts: 'Sat set sittin thur suppin'. He was already showing signs of becoming as mellow as a newt, but oozed kindliness and brown mixed from every pore. In response to his cheery vernacular greeting: "What's todo, feckler?", I hesitantly voiced my concern over the post-prandial billing.
"Oh, Aye, Reet," he explained with exaggerated and pained patience: "Number wun turn is a one-legged tap-dancer doing 'Knee-up Mother Brown' ... But not fur long! ... Number two turn is a dyslexic karaoke singer doing 'A you're a butterfly, B you're a custard pie ...' until he falls down drunk and chokes on 'is own Vimto. Number three turn ist speaker ... thee ... and number four turn ist comedian, Wandering Walter".

This proved to be a merely proximate forecast of the subsequent proceedings, but does give a fairly accurate rough guide to the relaxed zeitgeist of Wigan RLFC when letting their scrum-caps down.

The event was wondrously un-politically-correct, so I told my favourite Question of Sport, viz:-

Q. When did a Black Boxer after winning a world title urinate in the centre of the ring?
A. Crufts - 1979

Wandering Walter Horam's concluding spot was a lengthy analysis, in authentic Lancashire dialect, of his working life as an employee of Leyland Motors/British Leyland/Leyland Daf, ending with his account of an interview with Sir Michael Edwards, who boasted that: "Last year three of our apprentices broke a world record and built a Mini in nineteen minutes twenty-three seconds." To which Walter's laconic reply was: "Ay. An I bloody getten it!"

Here, as a gesture of thanks to Walter and Wigan is what the karaoke singer might have sung had he got past line two ...

DYSLEXIC DITTY.

A	you're a butterfly.
B	you're a custard pie.
C	is an ocean or a lake.
D	luxe describes your class.
E	you're a gradely lass.
F	ervescing like a con of cake.
G	U look marvellous.
H	makes uz proud of huss.
I	"ll never, ever, let us part.
J	did i'll never B.
K	sera sera U'll C.
L	th and beauty we'll share from the start.
MNOP	Our bliss will grow and grow.
QRST	dyslexically speaking you're K.O.
U	and me adds up to we.
V	will get on werrily
W	would fill my double bed.
X	tra close and loving care,
Y	s people long to share
	Right to the end, or down to Z.

In the original song, the ending was always wrong.
Cos Americans pronounce the Z as Zee.
But now I've been right through, the alphabet with U.
I'll stay forever, just U.C.

TOP-TABLE TERMAGANTS.

The Lady President at a diner of Tangent, which is the senior branch of Ladies Circle, equivalent to the 41 Club, or senior branch of Round Table, told me that they had voted to make me an Honorary Life Tangent. In my profuse thanks, I tentatively asked exactly what that meant. "I've no idea," she said, cranking her voice up one degree of poshness, as all Lady Presidents do on taking office, "but I think it means that you are a sort of elderly transvestite ... but don't worry the Duke of Edinburgh's one!"

Tangential Ladies make great dinner companions. They prefer stories rather than jokes, especially when they are about family, neighbours, schools, holidays and clothes. Like my story of the gentleman's outfitter measuring me for a new suit who asked me, more in pain than contempt, "May I enquire what Sir is going as?", or the Lady in the restaurant with a large brood squabbling over the menu who said in a loud voice: "If you can't pronounce it, we can't afford it!"

It is a myth that guests at formal functions, as in Officers' Messes and Gentlemen's Clubs, treat sex, politics and religion as taboo topics. Since saying Grace is still a normal part of most formal meals, it is not surprising that peripherally religious chat should often be used to break the ice. I am constantly reminded that among the most important words ever spoken are those which begin with the phrase: "And when they were at table ..."

For their balance of formality and fun, or gravity and levity, and for their ability to be serious without being solemn and frivolous without being fatuous, I have always enjoyed the company of the Ladies Luncheon Clubs. And I have a host of memories of simultaneously being wound-up and put-down by Lady Presidents. Like the one in Chester who asked: "Have you any family?", and when I replied that: "I have five women, aged sixteen, seventeen, eighteen, nineteen, and forty-three", peered over her pince-nez and growled: "Rather a large gap between the two eldest."

Then there was the lady in Birmingham who greeted me effusively: "And what are you going to talk to us about?" I replied in my best put-on Liverpool accent: "Scouse". "Oh, jolly good," she enthused: "I used to be a Ranger."

In Bristol, on one occasion, I was told by the boss Lady that her name was Brendal. "Yes, I remember being told," I boasted, "that if a word ends in a vowel, then Bristolians tend to put an 'el' on the end." "Not in this areal they don't," she corrected me. I decided that she was Swedish and was called Brendl. However, from then on she kept me guessing. They had recently been to the operal, she confided, or rather not a pukkal operal but a concert performance of Handel's Messial, spoiled by the behaviour of their secretary's children Idal and Eval, which was surprising because she was Normal ... and so on.

In Poole, I was once faced with a menu which listed 'Home Made Apple Pie' as the dessert. "Whose home was it made in?" I asked my hostess, in what I thought was light badinage. "You stupid man," she answered with some acerbity, "that means it's not out of a tin."

On occasions when the Top-Table-Terrors have been overwhelming, there have usually been diversions provided by the waitresses, like the one I overheard asking her friend: "Are the Vegans the ones with pointy ears?" Or the very starchy occasion when an elderly waitress approached the distinguished head of a multi-national corporation, dug him in the ribs, and announced in a loud Glaswegian accent: "A've bin a widder naw fer thiry-seven years ... an I'm 'on the prowl' tonight."

NOW ABOUT OUR CALENDAR

To control these memorable occasions there are nowadays, crimson-coated, Brunhilde-voiced Toastmistresses, as competent as their male counterparts at comforting the over-fortified and consoling the Lady Treasurer for the fact that the raffle prizes are so rotten that the people with the winning tickets won't own up. Not to mention regaling their hearers with such Pre-Reformation delights as: "Craving your indulgence ..."

CRAVEN INDULGENCE.

"Top Table remain, all the rest please depart.
Don't take your drinks with you, we're ready to start.
Yes, you've time for the toilet, it's on the next floor.
You can't get confused: it says GENTS on the door."
(That's our urinitarian settled at last!
This mob's getting restless, so better move fast.)

"Please line up in order, the gents on the right.
No, the toilet's downstairs, just go down the one flight.
Would the fraternal delegates please form a group.
The clasp has gone Madam, best walk with a stoop.
Yes, my Lord, try and hold out as long as you can.
The dress code said 'Formal' : you'd best sack your Man.

Quick, find your right places and follow my lead.
If you trip on the carpet, please try not to bleed.
No, my Lady forgive me, that's my little joke.
From now to the Loyal Toast try not to smoke.
If you just can't refrain, then at least be discreet.
There's a place set apart. It's four doors down the street.
Yes, Madam, that too was a rather poor gag."
(Where on earth did he find such a crabby old bag!)

"Now are we all ready, Lord President, Sir?
Lend a hand to our 'tired and emotional' Mayor.
When you see all the guests, try and keep a straight face,
And check your own buttons and flies, just in case.
Right off we all go, there's a card at each place.
Don't sit till the Bishop has finished the Grace."

(Now gods give me strength, and I promise I'll try
To remember that strong men don't break down and cry.)
"Pray, all be up-standing." (That's those who are able!)
"And welcome your host and his guests to top table.
I do hope you have an enjoyable night.
No, Sir, it's downstairs. Second door on the right."

BE STOOD UP.

One beautiful Summer's evening, I decided to walk from my hotel to the Guildhall, where I was to speak at a dinner of the Institute of Bankers. When I was half-way there, I was caught in a torrential downpour. The streets immediately became taxiless. I panicked and made a dash for it.

Arriving saturatedly, squelchingly sodden, I stood, dripping and breathless, at the door of the VIP reception-room. The Toastmaster looked me up-and-down, rapped on the lintel, and announced: "Mister President, Sir. There is a soggy person claiming acquaintance."

I was about to say something roughly translateable as: "Blow this for a game of bankers," when the President turned round, threw his arms out, guffawed with mirth and said: "Peter, how good to see you again. Let me get you a drink." Then, to the Toastmaster: "See if you can find us a large towel and a dry pair of socks." Then, to me again: "You know my wife, of course. Let me introduce you to some friends. There are some people here just dying to meet you."

By the time we had done the rounds, and I had changed my socks, it was time to go in to the banquet. There was a lively buzz, and dreadful-weather jokes were breaking the ice all around.

From that evening onwards, I have never had the slightest doubt that one day, after life's storms, I will find myself standing at the threshold of eternity. The Recording Angel will rap on the Pearly Gates and announce: Almighty Father, there is a sinful person claiming acquaintance."

After a painful silence, the Lord will turn to me, with outstretched arms and say: "Peter, how good to see you." Then He will send my Guardian Angel to get me a towel and clean socks. (Theologians call that process purgatory, but it's not a good name.) The Lord will then say to me: "You know My Mother, of course. Let me get you a glass of the new wine. There are some people here who have died to meet you."

As we enter the Heavenly Banquet, the Archangel will announce: "Enter into the joy of the Lord."

Anyone who thinks this is all a wild delusion has either never read the gospels and epistles, or is not a paid-up member of the Institute of Bankers.

CONSIDERED TRIFLES.

The Furniture Guild paid a fortune,
On food for their annual treat.
So the catering staff all decided.
To throw in a nice free pea sweet.

****

Finish up yer breakfast,
Dinna mak a fuss.
It's porridge to the Sassenachs.
But oat cuisine tae us.

****

"Eat up your onions, they make a man manly.
Who cares if your breath starts to smell?"
"It isn't the breath that's the problem with onions.
They make a boy boily as well."

****

JUST DESSERTS.

Miss Delia Smith wrote a cook-book.
The Queen said: "That sounds right for me.
It's called 'One Is Fun' so it must be."
Now she's Delia Smith O.B.E.

****

I've got a black belt for my cooking.
Or so say my children and wife.
It's marital arts at the Aga.
One chop and you're crippled for life.

****

"To operate on waitresses,"
The surgeon, said, "I am not able.
I'd love to help them, if I could.
But this is not my table.

NORTH-SOUTH DIVIDEND.

As with all absurd generalisations, there is a grain of truth in the assertion by chauvinist Northerners that whereas Southerners are mainly interested in things, Northerners are chiefly interested in people. Similarly, there is accuracy in the distinction made by music lovers that the South is for Chamber Ensembles and the North is for Brass Bands. Both consider themselves superior to Midlanders. I recall being welcomed to a civic function in Birmingham with the words: "Welcome to Britain's second greatest city." To which my Liverpool companion's puzzled response was: "I always thought that was London."

Bands seem to provide better stories than Ensembles. From the Salvation Army: "Thank you Madam, is there any particular hymn you would like?" "Ay, him on't big drum." To the story told in Northern Pennine territory of how Franz Lehar on a visit to this country, found himself in Nether Poppleton. On the door of the Church Hall he saw a poster advertising an Amateur Operatic Society performance of 'Good Night Vienna'. Vanity mingling with curiosity, he went into the hall and asked the Manager if 'Good Night Vienna' was proving popular in Nether Poppleton, only to receive the clear Northern reply: "'Appen, anyroad, it's rather more popular than 'Good Night Poppleton' would be in Nether Vienna."

The last time I heard a Franz Lehar medley was in a concert by the Thornleigh Salesian Silver Band in the Albert Hall, Bolton.

There was a more famous concert in the same venue which deserves to be remembered in Lancastrian verse:-

SCORE
BOLTON 3
MUSIC 0

BLOW THE WIND NORTHERLY.

In Albert Hall, Bolton, each Saturday night.
A brass band plays, right through the season.
But one night stands out, from the many there've been.
An that fer a very good reason.

They started with trombones, then softened the blow,
To trumpets, all playing 'Reveille'.
Then drums beat 'Retreat', which turned into a rout.
And ended-up down Tympannali.

I reckon twas Briggus, or Black Dyke Mills Band.
At anyroad it wur a good'un.
But 'im on the organ, a donor no doubt,
Went all Celtic-mad of a sudden.

We'd Highlands and Islands and Valleys and Hills
An a chorus ev 'Wild Irish Rover'.
Then came syncopation, which means 'bar-to-bar'.
And thence we went several times over.

Next, her on the flugelhorn switched to guitar,
An everyone started gyrating.
They wus rocking an rollin and jivin an all.
Consensus was: "Leave Bartok waiting".

So they ditched Shostakovich, and Elgar as well.
Left out Handel and Berlioz too.
It wasn't much cop as a concert, by heck.
But we all had a reet cracking 'do'.

EXEGETING OUT.

The youngster in the restaurant asking her Mummy: "Why are these pea-pods called 'Man Get Out?'", reminded me of the Anglican Bishop who complained to his dinner-host that he had been served: "The piece of cod that surpasseth all human understanding."

Puns and word-play can enhance our understanding and appreciation of texts which have become stale and boring. After ploughing through dozens of almost identical job -applications recently, I finally decided that the post should go to the man whose optimism was clearly better than his typing. His CV included a list of his 'educational smile-stones'. That took me back to the day some years ago when I asked an interviewee if he had a current CV: to which he replied: "Our firm doesn't give them. You have to bring a packed lunch".

There was a celebratory mass in the Liverpool Metropolitan Cathedral twenty years ago which included a troupe of dancing girls acting out the liturgy round the sanctuary in dance and mime. The event is fixed in my memory because towards the end of the mass a weary voice from the back of the congregation was heard to exclaim: "Take your partners for the last gospel". Younger readers will not know what the 'Last Gospel' was, but almost every pre-vat-two mass ended with the priest reading the opening of Saint John's gospel: "In principio erat verbum ... etc". The practice went back many centuries. Eight hundred years ago, Geoffrey Chaucer satirised priests of what we would call 'the Brylcreem tendency' whose recital of 'In Principio' was 'all so siker' ... that they always got a good collection: "Yet wolde he have a farthing!"

As a small altar-boy who had to carry the missal to the other side of the altar for the last gospel, I used to wonder what the 'Word' was that was 'with God' for I saw that 'verbum' was spelt with an ornamental capital 'V', and the text went on to say, even more bafflingly, that "the Word was God." Thankfully "the Word was made flesh and dwelt among us" took the text beyond mere semantics; made sense as a valedictory at the end of mass; and somehow sent everyone away with the conviction that being a Christian is not a matter of words, education, cleverness, knowledge, or general smarty-tude, but of making the words flesh: in family, in parish, in community.

It also heightened my poetic awareness of words in themselves. As the great Irish poet Yeats once said: "Some men believe in God, some say there is no God. The truth is probably in-between." In the ending is the Word?

AGNOSTIC IGNORAMUS.

Evolution's the gospel for men of today.
Religion's a thing of the past.
So ditch Deuteronomy, silence the psalms,
And pin God's white flag to the mast.

It's in Genome not Genesis answers are found
As to how our creation began.
A Big Bang of Nothing first started it off.
And, Lo and Behold, there was Man.

The scintilla of our synteresis is thought
To explain all transcendental joys,
In cultural recap of strand D.N.A.
Inherited as girls and boys.

There's an infinite space which is full of black holes.
All predicted by Einstein and Co.
And pararallel cosmosses where black is white,
Up is downwards, and quickly is slow.

Quantum physics mutatus with quasars and quarks,
Is the answer to evil and pain.
With sign-posts all pointing to nowhere at last,
For Heaven and Hell's in the brain.

Such theories can't be distilled in a lab.
It's hopeless, so better not try.
Our life-and-death questions remain unresolved.
So be careful and don't ever die!

JOLLY GSOH.

Not to have a sense of humour is to be a psychological cripple. I don't know whether people are born with it or develop it, nor how to compensate for its lack to those who don't have it.

If you have no sense of humour, then you cannot see disproportion in things, the absurdity of which is what makes us laugh. And so, you have no sense of proportion, or direction; you can't navigate, or lead, or educate, nor allow for the wind: of either change or dyspepsia.

I was once asked to speak to three separate groups at an international conference in the N.E.C. Birmingham, on the theme of: "The Place of Humour in Business."

To the first group, I began by saying: "No one who has ever seen a hippopotamus can deny that Almighty God has a sense of humour." The meeting quickly degenerated into wrangling about laughter and theology, in the style of The Name of the Rose.

To the second group, I began by saying: "In his book on Chaucer, G. K. Chesterton defines satire by saying that: "No one who has ever seen a hippopotamus can deny that Almighty God has a sense of humour." That meeting soon dissolved into literary arguments about Middle English Verse and Father Brown Stories.

To the third group, I began by saying: "To define satire, in his biography of Chaucer, Chesterton quoted verse twenty-six of psalm one hundred and four, which says that: 'No one who has ever seen a hippopotamus can deny that Almighty God has a sense of humour." Several of the delegates promptly sneaked out of the room, and I knew that they had gone up to their rooms to check the reference in their bed-side Gideon Bibles; where they read: "(Yahweh, what variety you have created) ... and Leviathan whom You made to amuse you."

Which enabled me to make the necessary distinction between having a sense of humour and being able to tell jokes. Like the one about the man in the Birmingham hotel who read, scribbled in his Gideon Bible: "If you have a problem with alcohol, ring ..." followed by a local phone number. Sober, but curious, he rang, only to find himself talking to the manger of an off-licence in the Bull-ring.

The Brits have always prided themselves on their GSOH, as well as their love of free-speech, their NHS, the Welfare/Nanny State, a voracious appetite for poetry and the youthfulness of their Bobbies.

As English becomes a universal language, so Englishness becomes more fascinating to the rest of the world. The signs and symbols of our culture are mostly taken from old films and new travellers. If cycling from the pub to Evensong, past the cricketers on the village green, is no longer what it was; there are still certain enduring signs of what it means to be Made in England.

Had that most English of poets, William Blake, lived for another couple of centuries, he might have sung the praises of a Community Police Officer in a Song of Innocence and Experience like:

AND PLOD THOSE FEET

People's Peeler from the Met,
With our short-wave radio set.
You don't know which way to go,
Cos yer 'at comes down too low.

Stop and search the likes of us.
Using guess-work; call it 'suss'.
No time left to tackle toughs.
Too weighed down with torch and cuffs.

Call for back-up from the Bill.
Or the Sweeney, that's a thrill.
PC- this and DC-that,
On the mobile for a chat.

Operation 'Plates of meat',
For your fabled outsize feet.
Get on Crimewatch. Study hard.
Your two feet might make the Yard.

MAL VOYAGE.

All seasoned travellers have favourite horror stories. Here are some of my favourites of bicycle, car, aeroplane and railway. Followed by the poem which Masefield might have written about the London Underground. First, a true confession of a cycling malefaction.

I have a criminal record. Well, more of a criminal flip-side really. I was on a Student Cross Pilgrimage to Walsingham. One of the pilgrims sprained an ankle and I was deputed to use our emergency bicycle to carry him, on the crossbar, to the nearest town, to find a doctor. We were apprehended by an officer of the Melton Mowbray fuzz, who was not amused by our subtle jokes about cross-bearing, and was clearly looking forward to the headline in the local rag: ZERO TOLERANCE BLITZ ON PIE TOWN CRIME WAVE. I treasured my notice of conviction for many years. As did my partner in crime, now a distinguished Manchester Doctor. It recorded that there was imposed on us: "A fine of ten shillings, for being each of one of two persons riding upon a mechanically-propelled vehicle not adapted for the carrying of two persons, to whit a bicycle, in the environs ..."

It being a Sunday, we had difficulty finding a doctor who would answer the door. Eventually we roused a fierce Scottish lady who greeted us; "Do ye no ken it's the Sabbath?"

She ignored our query; " And is it not lawful to heal on the Sabbath?" and bound up the offending ankle after twisting and twirling it unmercifully for ten minutes in an exercise in sadism that she described as; "Listening for crepitus". If crepitus includes swearing, she was amply rewarded!

My favourite traffic-cop story tells of a woman who was pulled up on the M25 doing a ton. The policeman who pulled her over formed the opinion that she was intoxicated, and cautioned her: "Madam, you don't have to say anything, But whatever you do say will be taken down and I will read it out in court." To which she replied: "Please don't hit me again, with your truncheon."

Back to true tales. I was on an overnight flight once, when the Captain woke us up with the announcement: "Ladies and Gentlemen, we will be arriving in Manchester twenty minutes early. This is entirely due to the incredible skill of the crew."

For PR skill, that is almost matched by the conductor of the laughingly titled Trans-Pennine Express who explained an unscheduled stop at Guide Bridge with the message: "Ladies and Gentlemen, De train am stop again. De reason dis time is ..." and after a long pause ... "Human cock-up."

TUBE FEVER.

Six a.m. from Ickenham, near distant Uxbridge,
Coming in to Baker Street, by way of Wembley Park.
Crammed full with early birds, city gents and office girls.
Scrambling off the platforms in the eerie morning dark.

Mid-morning rush-hour, chaos at Victoria,
Similar at King's Cross. Same at Waterloo.
From Heathrow and Gatwick, the Chunnel and the Mainline.
Apologies for cancelled trains, and signal failures too.

Exodus at eventide, back to leafy suburbs.
Theydon Bois or Ruislip, all the way past Hangers Lane.
With standing-room only to Mile End or Shepherds' Bush.
'Mind the gap' and 'Clear the doors' and 'Move right down the train'.

Evening-time brings revellers, mixed with groups of school-kids,
Stayed out playing football, now reluctant to go home.
Crowds from the Circle Line, or the Metropolitan:
Changing from the Jubilee: ill-fated since the Dome.

Last tube out of Holborn. No late trains from Aldwych.
Buskers, drunks and sleepers-rough, who can't get out of town.
Posses of bill-posters, round the stairs at Bond Street.
Smokers having one last drag, before they are sucked down.

BELIEVING INSANITY CLAUSE.

To demonstrate to aspiring thespians the difference between drama, melodrama and farce, I used to quote the dialogue from Dickens' A Christmas Carol, as performed by a school drama group, consequent on the appearance of the ghost of Jacob Marley.

Scrooge: "Who are you?" (That's drama.)
Ghost: "Ask me rather who I was?" (That's melodrama.)
Scrooge: "Alright, 'oo was you then?" (That's farce.)

The modern equivalent of a Dickensian Christmas Story would feature the little lad in the grotto who marched up to Father Christmas, punched him on the nose and announced: "That's for last year."

Or, perhaps it would re-tell the tale of the liberal Jewish Father, in the East End of London, who said to his sons on Christmas Eve: "Tonight, kinder, you hang up your stockings. During the night, Judas Maccabeus will come down the chimney, wake you up, and ask: 'Who wants to buy a present'."

I once compered a Liverpool Primary Schools Christmas concert at which the Narrator was so carried away that he ended the nativity narrative with the lovely words: "An even the Angels was that made up, thee was all singen and dancen."

I also once chaired a business conference in late December at which the local newspaper proudly proclaimed that: "Lord King of B.A is to be made MANGER OF THE YEAR." I had to restrain myself from singing the song about Bruno the Black-eyed Reindeer, who's as fast as Rudolph but can't pull up as quickly.

The serious message behind all such stories is that a word is never as important as the Word made Flesh, and people who deal in words are never as valuable as people who make the words flesh, in families, in schools, in communities.

So, if, as Jung said: "The eternal child in man is what decides the ultimate worth of a personality", then every child should be able to celebrate a Christmas, a Chanuka, or a Diwali.

THE HOLY AND THE POISON-IVY.

"You are old Father Christmas, "the young man said,
"And your myth has become very stale.
Do you think it is right to bamboozle the kids,
With such an improbable tale?"

"In my youth," said Saint Nicholas, through his white beard,
"I started the Santa Claus story.
And now I am more than contented to find,
The tradition persistent, though hoary."

"You are old," said the youth, "As I mentioned before.
And your 'Ho-Ho' is now very trite.
Yet you still lure the kids, with your grotto and glitz.
In this age, could it really be right?"

"In my day," said the Saint, "I collected the gifts
Of the rich to pass on to the poor.
And whether by grotto, or giro, or crib,
I'm glad it gets done more and more."

"You are old and deceitful," the cynic then scoffed.
With your Lapland, and Fairies and Gnomes.
Pretending to ride with your reindeer and sleigh,
Down chimneys, right into folks' homes.

"Oh, get a life, Sonny," the old Saint advised.
"And stop being bitter and sad.
Give thanks to your Maker, for Christmas, with joy.
And celebrate, there's a good lad."

STRESS AND DISTRESS.

"Absence of stress is called 'Death'", might have been what that great bon-mower George Bernard Shaw was thinking when he said that; "Every day I perform two acts of heroic virtue. I get up and I go to bed."

Stress is good. It fuels our every waking activity. It oils the wheels of our relationships. It elicits empathy. It directs motivation. Superfluous stress, or the wrong stress for our specifically-desired activities or relationships, is DIStress. But the distress that causes anger, frustration and depression is quite different from the absence of stress.

Many doctors' surgeries are crowded with people who can't cope with the absence of stress. Too little stress leads to boredom and hypochondria. It is characteristic of unemployment and imprisonment, as well as of invalidity and immobility.

Actuaries, the profession defined as being: "Those who can't stand the excitement of accountancy", assure us in their gambling-tables of morbidity that retired teachers have a lower life-expectancy than the general population. This is because teachers' working lives are spent surrounded by hundreds of little stresses: a process that has been likened to being: "Nibbled to death by ducks", or in the case of religious schools of being: "Pecked to death by doves".

Take away the STRESSES of their lives and all that is left are the STRAINS of Auld Lang Syne.

In my experience of chairing conferences of widely differing groups, there has always been a dynamic tension between the happy stress of the high-flying achievers, and the sad distress mediated by some of the less well-motivated subordinates, partners or bosses.

We should rejoice in all the stresses we are able to put to work for ourselves and others, but beware of how, when, and on to whom, we off-load our distress.

If reading this pulls you up-tight short, you might enjoy the following verse, which summarises a psychiatrist's current case-list

SICKIATRIC NUT-CASE-STUDIES.

There's an exile from South Africa, in post Natal depression,
Who takes PMTea in Downing Street, if parliament's in session.

And a man who laid a psychopath instead of crazy paving.
With a raver from a disco-club, in ecstacy and raving.

There are groggy merchant seamen who are hard-a-port and aleing.
Trailed by Anna Bollick Steroid, who keeps taking tests and failing.

Reading verses by McGough entitled 'Physio The rapist'.
To an Ulster ecumaniac called Doctor Ian Papist.

And the love-lorn poker gambler with a busted-flush in hearts.
With his trumped-up dummy partner doubling as the Queen of Tarts.

Or the PC PC artist at a painted scene of crime.
With an anon alcoholic lurching twelve steps at a time.

To an RAC patrol-car with a nervous breakdown driver.
Whose psyche is dysfunctional an can't fink proper neiver.

Then an anorexic Oliver who keeps demanding less.
With the Bunter of Bulimia all puke-u-like and mess.

A dyslexic Christmas Devil who stole toys from Satan's grotto.
For a girl who gave up Bingo when she started getting Blotto.

Some Women from the Institute who run a nudist choir.
And sing all night of burning bows and arrows of desire.

Then there's sex-war-syndrome sufferers with hormones all upset.
And the victims of gross negligence by doctor and by vet.
They're a splendid source of income which has never dried up yet

TEAM-WORK.

The most popular buzz-word at conferences for the past ten years has been 'team-work'. However, requests for presentations on this theme have almost always come from those at the top of the relevant hierarchy, making them sound like the condescending aristocrat assuring members of the great unwashed that: "There is no need to call me 'Sir' my good man!"

To illustrate the dangers inherent in team-work, I like the story which tells how hundreds of dockers were pulling a ship into dock on a long thick rope when suddenly the rope snapped, but not one of them fell over.

More up-lifting, and challenging, is the cautionary story told by Jean Vanier, the French Canadian founder of L'Arche. He was teaching Indian children and set them a problem while promising a fantastic reward to the first to give the right answer. To his surprise they all got up and went outside, where they argued it out until they were sure they had the right answer and then came back, sat down, and all shouted out the correct answer together. Vanier poses the question as to whether he was more civilised or more savage than they were.

He might also have asked the wider question as to the difference between enlightened self-esteem and predatory self-esteem, which team leaders and Captains of Industry so often ignore, to their cost. Native Canadians, descended from generations of hunters and warriors, know that being able to trust those on your flanks is a matter of life and death. Cabinets and corporations that neglect this truth quickly find themselves out-flanked.

My favourite paradigm for team-workers is an orchestra, which is a splendid example of harmony produced from diversity. Separate sections, using a variety of instruments, playing from different scores, pursuing individual and group standards of excellence, produce a beautiful, and profitable, end-product.

Provided, that is, that practice has been rigorous and conscientious, that there are good section leaders, and that they work with a conductor whom they all trust implicitly, and whose esteem has been earned and not merely ascribed.

REVERENTIA AD VERSES SENEX?

Being a long-time fan and supporter of the 'Dead Poets' Society', I thought, when I started teaching English, that I knew how to teach poetry. I knew all the classic definitions of poetry by the poets themselves and the critics and had my own definition, which is: 'Poetry is any communication that MEANS more than it SAYS.'

Teaching West African School Certificate in Eastern Nigeria made me realise how narrow were my supposed insights. The English syllabus included William Shakespeare alongside Chinua Achebe, and William Wordsworth together with Wole Soyinka. On special occasions the students would cheerfully and energetically act out scenes from A School For Scandal, complete with 'O lud Mam's' and 'business' with imaginary spinnets and powdered wigs, followed by 'The Death of Patrice Lumumba' with fervent gravitas.

When our daughter Catherine was just a few weeks old, she had a severe bout of malaria. A Sister of the Medical Missionaries of Mary from the Mission Hospital in Ikom gave her an injection of resochin and advised that: "All you can do now, is pray."

I felt desperate and useless, and hence guilty. When 'siesta time' came, I left the house and wandered round the school compound, finishing up in my office. There, I grabbed a book from the shelf and opened it at random. It was the poetry set-text for that year and was called: 'Ten Twentieth-Century Poets.' The poem at which it fell open was by John Betjeman and was entitled: 'A Child ill.'

Sensing, if not an answer to prayer, at least an affinity of pain, I stayed all afternoon reading and re-reading:

> O little body, do not die.
> The soul looks out through wide blue eyes,
> So questioningly into mine,
> That my tormented soul replies:
> O little body do not die.
> You hold the soul that speaks to me,
> Although our conversation be
> As wordless as the windy sky'.
> So looked my father, at the last,
> Right in my soul, before he died.
> Though words he spoke went heedless past,
> As London traffic roar outside.

87

And now the same blue eyes I see,
Look through me from a little son.
So questioning, so searchingly,
That youthfulness and age are one.
My father looked at me, and died,
Before my soul made full reply.
Lord, leave this other light alight.
O little body, do not die.

I am quoting it now from memory, thirty-five years on. It may not be entirely accurate because I have never read it since, and this is how it is imprinted on my soul. Later, looking back on this episode, I arrogantly thought that at last I had learned the true meaning of poetry, and the truth of Wordsworth's claim that it must be: "Felt in the pulse and felt along the heart."

However, twenty years later, I was asked to 'do a spot on the Late Late Show' for Telefis Eireann in Dublin. It was at short notice but I had worked before with Gay Byrne, both over here at Granada and in Dublin, so I accepted the invitation. To my surprise and delight the guest immediately preceding me on the show was John Betjeman. To my dismay, though, I heard Gay Byrne say to him: "Lots of people think you are not a 'proper' poet but just a versifier." Or words to that effect. Gentle, courteous Englishman that he was, Betjeman made a non-commital reply and then Gay introduced me as a supporting Anglo-visitor. I immediately professed my opinion that: "Far from being a mere versifier, John Betjeman writes great and beautiful poetry." "Such as?", queried our host. And so, I told the story about Catherine which I have told above, and started to recite: "Oh, little body do not die ..."

As I did so, Betjeman started to cry. As he wept gently, there was the most profound silence that I have ever heard in a theatre, and when I finished, the stillness continued and the camera stayed focussed on John's tears. Finally, I managed to say: "That is great and beautiful poetry." Betjeman nodded, and added: "I couldn't have recited it like that."

I said: "I'm sorry it brought back sad memories of your dead son."
"Oh, he didn't die," he answered, "he's alive and well and living in (I think) Cambridge. What about your daughter?"

"She's alive and well, and studying at Oxford."

The discussion moved on, and it was only afterwards that I realised that a poet had shown us what poetry really is.

And does.

SHUFFLING OFFER.

A quaint conjunction of mathematics and theology was recently presented to me by a misprint which turned the contents of an article which I was writing for a religious journal into an essay about St. Atistics. Had there been such a person, I would have been praying to him as I approached my seventieth birthday, since everyone kept assuring me that three-score-years-and-ten is my allotted span: "According to biblical statistics."

I have distrusted statistics since I first heard the FBI story of the Kerryman arrested at Boston airport carrying a crude home-made bomb. Charged with endangering an aircraft, he claimed in his defence that he was actually increasing the life-expectancy of all the passengers, and produced a book of statistics to support his claim. "The odds against there being a bomb on a plane," he quoted, "are twenty-one thousand to one against. The odds against there being two bombs on a plane are a million to one against. So I take a bomb along with me to lengthen the odds." That's both a parable about statistics and a fable about mortality. Rather like Aneurin Bevan's claim that he would not die happy; "Until everyone in the country earns more than the average wage."

Shortly after my sixty-fifth birthday, an insurance salesman called on me. He gleefully showed me a 'Table of Mortality'. I told him that "Table of Mortality' sounds like a euphemism for 'Mortuary Slab', and that the only two certainties are death and taxis and neither of them comes when you want it. I added that what the great Jesuit poet, Gerard Manley Hopkins, called "the incomprehensible certainties" are not capable of statistical anaylsis. He produced a Whole-of-Life Policy that seemed to me to be more of a Hole-in-Wallet Policy and said that I: "Owed it to my better half." This reminded me of an old joke about Anglican Bishops having a better half, while Catholic Bishops have better quarters, so I signed up and agreed to have a full medical check-up. I duly took myself off to my GP. A week later, after blood tests, X-rays, specimen analysis, bodily palpation and neurological investigation, he delivered his verdict. Without benefit of Mortality Tables, he pronounced: "Given your life-style, body-mass-ratio, genetic-profile and histo-pathology you have between twenty-five and forty percent chance, within the next ten years of having a morbid coronary episode." For which I was grateful, since I had feared he was going to tell me the odds against my having a heart attack! He rather spoiled it by adding that the insurers required details about my next-of-kin, which made me feel like the trance-medium in the Benchley New Yorker cartoon saying to the circle of hand-holding clients at a seance: "There's a horse here that wants to say 'Hello'."

As a parting shot, the doctor reminded me, with a guffaw, that: "Life depends on the liver." I smugly added that: "Eternal life depends on the dier." He asked me what I thought eternal life would consist of, and so I showed him the obituaries in the copy of the local newspaper I was still carrying from the waiting-room. "Obviously, most people think it consists of reading excruciatingly bad doggerel verse," I said. "Ah, yes," he replied, nodding sagely, "I had heard that you were rather good at that."

What are the odds that Hopkins never had to deal with such nerds?

Anyway, what's wrong with GOOD doggerel verse?

MIS-NAMING OF PARTS.

"A bullet is lodged in her yet," it said.
Not in her what, when or how.
It must have dis-rupted her then, I suppose,
But won't cause much pain in her now.

****

THREE TRIES AND CONVERSION.

"His industry, my ministry, supported by psychiatry,
Are reasons why my client here
Is asking for judicial pardon.
As God gave Adam, it's quite clear,
When he offended in the Garden."

"Let me remind, my Learned Friend,
To tell his client clearly how,
God only answered Adam's pleas,
After his fierce domestic row,
When he stopped hiding in the trees."

GRAND FATHER TIME.

I never knew my paternal Grandfather, who was a piper from the West of Ireland who brought his family to Liverpool at the beginning of the last century. His pipes are still on show in the folk museum in Dublin. The boys in the family became doctors and the girls teachers like my Grandmother. And like my maternal Grandfather and Grandmother.

When I was a small boy, I thought that my other Victorian Headmaster of a Grandfather was a bombastic, bumptious old pedant. Now that I am a Grandfather myself, I'm absolutely certain that he was.

He would sit in his personal armchair wearing polished lace-up boots and/or spats and starched wing collar. He would then talk, or rather pontificate, over the heads of his grandchildren, using irritatingly coded language, like the adults in David Copperfield talking about: "Mister Brooks of Sheffield."

He it was who first made me interested in wordplay. Though not intentionally. I had just been given my first Junior Pocket Dictionary. The following day I was sitting at his feet and he was quizzing me, as was his wont. He would promise me a 'funny coin' i.e. one of the old threepenny bits, if I answered his questions correctly. However, if I did answer correctly he would roll his eyes to the adults and mutter: "A little knowledge is a dangerous thing." If I could not answer correctly he would say quite bafflingly: "Alas, no 'out of the mouths of babes and sucklings' here." In either event, no coin was forthcoming. Funny or otherwise.

On this occasion, after he had gone off for his lunch, I stayed listening to his wireless. Suddenly he re-appeared, strode over to where I was sitting and snapped off the wireless with a snort of: "That strumpet!". Thinking that a strumpet must be some sort of diabolical musical instrument, like the virginals floating down the river Thames which I had read of in my Junior Edition of Pepys' Diary, I scuttled off home to consult my dictionary. Sadly, the word 'strumpet' was clearly too Senior, so I had to ask my Father. He gave me a number of synonyms, none of which I understood, and then asked me where I had come across the word. I explained about Old Man Geraghty, as my Father used to call him, and asked whether the 'strumpet' was Gracie Fields, who was singing, or Sally, the 'girl in our alley' who was the subject of her song. My Father thought long and hard and then explained that Gracie Fields had just married a famous trumpeter called Archie, and that O.M.G. was probably making a joke about his signature tune which was called 'Strumpet Voluntary'.

Years later, I discovered the truth, and remembered that where words were concerned O.M.G. never ever made a joke, whereas my father never ever didn't.

I went and bought a bigger dictionary.

AD VERSE REPORTS.

I've now got nine points on my poetic licence.
When it reaches to twelve I'll be bard.
To stick to the rules for the reading of metres
Is terpsichoreicly hard.

With a proud pedigree as a poet from childhood,
Whose cries, yells and screams used to scan.
It caused no surprise when I later turned into
An oxymoronical man.

My mother was crippled by iambic feet.
And descended from quite a long line.
My father was said to be more anapaestic,
From over-indulgence in wine.

A life doomed to prose is a sentence of death.
Or terrible phrase at the least.
And nearly as bad as a World-Wide-Web E-Male:
A sad metaphorical beast.

I'm guilty of assonance and sussuration,
With alliteration or worse.
A habit derived from the great Doctor Spooner.
Ideal for varrative nurse.

If the long arm of interplod queries my scansion,
Alleging syntactical crime.
I'll have to refrain from reversing my quatrains,
While leaving the scene of the rhyme.

MEMORIAM MORATORIUM.

If these reminiscences have been sublimely absurd, and have been punctuated by lapses from the beautiful banal and assinine arcane into what Star Trek fans might call Holo-deck Theology, then they are probably a fair reflection of my life. Or even of everybody's life, which ends for all of us in new life beyond the grave. Or a parallel universe of anti-matter through the worm-hole?

Any attempt to balance gravity and levity usually leaves us floating in space, or wandering lonely as a cloud, which is why I have laced my prosaic narrative with exalted lapses into verse, in the hope that the words would be empowered to mean more than they say.

What Trekkies most enjoy are flights of the imagination, which William Blake described as: "The Holy Ghost in Everyman." Mind you, an alien visiting our world might well be forgiven for thinking that we believe that part of the joy of the Blessed Departed consists in reading local newspapers. I am a keen supporter of local newspapers and heart-felt doggerel, because bad doggerel can make good prayers. And vice versa. In our school chapel, whenever we sang: "We send up our sighs ..." there was always a murmured afterthought ... "six and three-quarters ..." I once attended a near-empty cathedral, during a bus strike, where the opening hymn was: "Lord, let this transport last ..." and I often heard the story of the dramatic consequences of the Curate's announcement at the wedding "During the signing of the register, the choir will sing the old Negro Spiritual: 'Carry me back to Old Virginity.'

I can personally vouch for the truth of one hymnodic highlight of the Pope's visit to this country. The throng gathered at Liverpool's Speke Airport awaiting the Holy Father's arrival heard an announcement by the police, over the tannoy system, warning everyone to be on their guard against pick-pockets. This was followed immediately by another voice which announced: "The choir will now sing the Old Negro Spiritual: "Steal Away."

One of my father's favourite stories was of attending the death-bed of Father Andrew, a Franciscan friar, who died on the feast of his patron saint. His last words were: "Beam me up, Scotty."

"The rest," as they say, "was well deserved."

UNCOMMON SENSE.

How many senses do I have?
Sight, hearing, touch, taste, smell.
How many others might there be?
Who knows? Or who can tell?

Do Angels have five different ones?
Is so, how could we know?
Unless some senses up above,
Were shared down here below.

They might be senseless messengers.
Their name says so in Greek.
Then they could act upon our souls,
Without the need to speak.

What we don't have, can we deny?
Like worms dismissing sight.
Or rather can we reach through them
To Uncreated Light?

Can Cherubim and Seraphim,
Protect us, in disguise?
And bring God's gifts to those who seek.
The simple, who are wise?

"Angel of God, my guardian dear,"
I hear the children say.
Have I the sense to senseless be,
And join them when I pray?

END-PEACE.

The proverb that says: "Death is nature's own way of warning us to slow down" was probably coined by the Scotsman who whenever he felt sick immediately sent for the undertaker because he: "Didnae believe in dealing wi middle-men."!

He would not have elicited the compassion wasted on a job-applicant who wrote in the box marked: "Father's occupation ..." the touching word: 'Dying' when what he meant was 'Dyeing.'

It is recorded that some years ago, on Merseyside, there was a strike of grave-diggers and crematorium workers, and a consequent spate of panic dying. At about the same time, there appeared on the gate-post leading into Anfield Cemetery the sublime chalked message: 'Sunday Eleven O'clock. Hearse Boot-Sale.'

I don't find that in the least 'mortifying' but rather up-lifting; like the experience of a friend at a 'wake' who was approached by a lady with the lovely words: "The corpse's brother asked 'Would you like a cup of tea?'" That is very much in the spirit of the Memoriam to: 'Lucy. Whose price was above Ruby's.' Or even of the contortionist who had a coronary on-stage and died in his own arms.

Which, in turn, is close to the spirit of the head-stone in the cemetery at Splott, in Cardiff, on which is written:

As the years roll onwards,
And memories grow dim.
We promise that, forever,
We shall remember her.

The original name for Splott was 'God's plot' which is a beautiful name for a grave-yard. And that head-stone is only rivalled in sublimity by the one for the Leeds nun, which should have read: "Sister Mary Aquinas. Requiescat in Pace. She was Thine.' But, owing to a misunderstanding, it actually read: 'Sister Mary Aquinas. Requiescat in Pace. She was thin.' Mother Superior complained to the mason: "You've left an E off the last line." He promised to replace the stone 'free of charge'. Which he duly did; with one that read: 'Sister Mary Aquinas. Requescat in Pace. Ee she was thin.'

All of which reinforces the truth that for Christians: "Death is swallowed up in victory."